# Praise for *Beyond Dalit Theology*

"Pulikottil writes not only on behalf of Dalits but as one convinced that Christian theology is true to its claims when it is fully public and socially transformative, so that what emerges is a theological method in action, exemplifying how the power of the gospel can and should make a difference in the real world."

—Amos Yong, dean, School of Mission and Theology,
Fuller Theological Seminary, Pasadena, California

"This book continues a tough, yet engaged, conversation in which probing questions are asked, enduring issues and themes looked at again, the gains of forty years reexamined, and current topics identified, all in the service of recognizing and reaffirming Dalit theology as relevant and responsive public theology amidst the chaotic realities of life today, wherever and with whomsoever we live, work, study, and worship at the frontiers of our commitment to upholding the humanity of all God's children."

—J. Jayakiran Sebastian, dean and H. George Anderson Professor
of Mission and Cultures, United Lutheran Seminary,
Gettysburg and Philadelphia

"Paulson Pulikottil has convincingly argued that if Dalit theology is to have real traction in India, it needs to go beyond advocating structural changes; it needs to be a theology that seeks the transformation of Christians, individually and corporately, by the power of the Spirit in and through the church. Only with a robust pneumatology and ecclesiology can there be a more holistic and enduring liberation. Here is a constructive theology that takes Dalit theology beyond its current stalemate."

—Simon Chan, editor of *Asia Journal of Theology*, Singapore

"There is a twofold task for *Beyond Dalit Theology*, namely to provide a constructive critique of this Indian liberation theology after the first four decades of its existence, as well as to chart a way towards a wider, more comprehensive vision of integral transformation. This work brings to the task vast and diverse resources, including ecclesiology, pneumatology, Christology, public theology, and societal analysis. Writing as a sympathetic outside critic, yet firmly located within the Indian society, church, and academia, the author calls the church to be faithful to her calling in facilitating transformation also in the society, not only within her own walls."

—Veli-Matti Kärkkäinen, professor of systematic theology,
Fuller Theological Seminary, Pasadena, California,
and docent of ecumenics, University of Helsinki

"This book is an invitation to expand the horizon of the hitherto existing Dalit theology to make it a promising theology of integral transformation. It is indeed an invitation to make Dalit theology effective in a substantive and abiding manner. Public theology is the key to make it happen, and Paulson Pulikottil makes a serious proposal in this regard. The book helps students of theology to explore some vital aspects of Indian public theology, which is very much in its birth-pangs today."

—Gnana Patrick, professor and head of the Department of Christian Studies,
School of Philosophy and Religious Thought, University of Madras

"Pulikottil has had the courage to look again at Dalit theology. The result is fresh and exciting, if perhaps controversial for some. The concept of 'integral transformation' considers the stage after 'liberation' of the oppressed. Liberation does not guarantee the right to live in a just and equitable society. How does one make societies more just, equitable? While the work focuses on the experience of the Dalit of India, the implications of this rethinking are applicable to all of Christian theology. The chains come off, and then what? This volume is an important contribution to the discipline of World Christianity as well as Dalit and Pentecostal studies."

—David Bundy, associate director, Manchester Wesley Research Centre,
Manchester, UK

# Beyond Dalit Theology

# Beyond Dalit Theology

*Searching for New Frontiers*

**Paulson Pulikottil**

Fortress Press
Minneapolis

BEYOND DALIT THEOLOGY
Searching for New Frontiers

Cover image: *Dalit Madonna*, by Jyoti Sahi, oil on canvas, 2000, from the Methodist
Modern Art Collection
Cover design: Savanah Landerholm

Print ISBN: 978-1-5064-7885-2
eBook ISBN: 978-1-5064-7886-9

*To my grandchildren: Arya, Anya, Mico, and Appu*

# Contents

# Preface

The motivation for this project came from my colleagues and friends who were engaged in Dalit theology and allied disciplines. Curiosity and the quest to extend my own boundaries of knowledge on the subject are the other reasons.

This book is the product of the third and last one-year sabbatical that I enjoyed during the two decades of my tenure at the Union Biblical Seminary, Pune, India. I am indebted to the ScholarLeaders International (SLI) and Langham Partnership for their support during the sabbatical. SLI funded my fellowship at the Centre for South Asia Research (CSAR) at the South Asia Institute of Advanced Christian Studies (SAIACS), Bengaluru. The Langham Partnership supported me as a Scholar in Residence at Ridley Hall, Cambridge, England, which facilitated access to the vast resources in the Cambridge University Library.

I am indebted to a lot of people, foremost my wife, Sheela. The sabbatical was a stressful period for us where our faith in God was tested and our patience saw its limits. But her support, along with the rest of my family, made this possible and to "count . . . all joy" (James 1:2) until the end.

I am indebted to everyone at Fortress Press, especially to Dr. Jesudas Athyal, for his interest and support of this project. The church I pastor, the Community of the Redeemed in Pune, stood with me as well.

# Introduction

There once was a dirty old sailor
Whose ship he began to abhor
The sails wouldn't budge
They moved like a sludge
Until a maid handed him an oar.[1]

A ship that has entered the doldrums sits still on a vast sheet of placid waters. There is no wind on the sails. There is calm: a painful, disturbing calm, since the hope of reaching the destination becomes bleaker as the days go along. The sailors lose their spirit, and the cargo begins to rot. That is when the sailors need oars to take the ship out of the lull to where there is wind to propel it farther. As it moves out of the doldrums, it will face turbulence on its course. But that is more desirable than being stuck in one place. Though the ship sometimes sails through troubled waters, nevertheless it is sailing toward new horizons. This metaphor is true of any academic discipline, including Dalit theology—being stagnant, getting out of it, moving forward, or being abandoned altogether is not new to any branch of human knowledge.

Dalit theology emerged on the theological horizons with tall masts, wide sails, and favorable winds in the early part of the 1980s. It captured the imagination of the burgeoning Indian theological enterprise. Though it had a commanding presence for decades, at least some sailors are concerned if it has entered the doldrums.

There are many reasons Dalit theology had a very imposing presence in the Indian theological landscape. First, the timing of its emergence was perfect. Theological education in India was taking new turns and twists in the

---

1 I found this little poem on an internet page that no longer exists. The poet, who signed as CP, is otherwise unknown.

1980s. In 1989, the South Asia Theological Research Institute (SATHRI) boasted homegrown research programs at the graduate and doctoral levels. Many new theological colleges being established around this time had an increased interest in theological inquiry. Besides, all the new theological journals published in India offered opportunities for Indian scholars to publish within India and for the Indian audience.

Second, Dalit theology emerged in an intellectual milieu of many similar movements, from which it drew sustenance and thrust. When it arrived on the scene, theological movements akin to it were already present on the Christian theological landscape. For example, liberation theology, with similar goals, was already onstage in Latin America, South Africa, and other places. Dalit theology has some kindred feelings with Black theology and Minjung theology. Black theology, which shares many features with Dalit theology, was already well established in North America and other parts of the world. Minjung theology, which challenged social and economic disparities, has already emerged in South Korea. Thus when Dalit theology emerged, it had these older movements to inspire it and to emulate. Moreover, no one could question its validity, since similar movements were already validated and accepted by the academy. As similar theological movements had already taken to the same waters, Dalit theology had only to join the fleet to sail the charted route.[2]

The third reason is related to the second. Dalit theology followed the theological shift that was gaining wide acceptance globally. The theological enterprise had turned its focus to contextual concerns from universalistic and dogmatic approaches. This implies that when Dalit theology arrived on the scene, it was part of the various theological innovations that theologians were experimenting with. The novelty of its concerns and approaches attracted the minds of Indian theologians who were craving new experiments and explorations. No doubt it gained a lot of momentum in its beginning. So with all these winds and currents in its favor, Dalit theology began its cruise toward new horizons.

There were critics and well-wishers of the enterprise. Halfway through, some concealed their disappointment and hoped that Dalit theology would continue in the right direction. For example, almost three decades

---

2  For a survey of the theologies that emerged in the Global South, including India, see John Parratt, ed., *An Introduction to Third World Theologies* (Cambridge: Cambridge University Press, 2004).

into its history, Jayakiran Sebastian points out that it has an unfinished agenda. In his own words, "Although so much has been achieved, including major interventions in the field of Biblical studies and hermeneutics and the rediscovery of Dalit literature, there is much that still needs to be done in the field of Dalit theology."[3]

The main objective of Dalit theology that it shared with its older siblings was the liberation of the oppressed Dalits in India, so it was rightly hailed as the Indian liberation theology.[4] Some authors prefer to call it "Dalit liberation theology," but I would rather stick to the shorter form—Dalit theology—but liberation is certainly implied.

My primary objective is not limited to critiquing Dalit theology; rather, I aim to explore the nature and content of a theology for integral transformation in India. Evaluating Dalit liberation theology is an essential part of this project. I hope a fresh assessment of Dalit theology will provide some useful lessons to guide us to the future. I will use lessons so learned in the second part to propose ways in which the Christian witness could be effective in transforming a society ridden with corruption, poverty, exploitation, and suffering—in other words, how the Christian gospel can bring the kingdom of God into the lives of the suffering millions in India.

I use the phrase *integral transformation* with caution. The word *liberation* presumes slavery or bondage. The task of Christian theology is not limited to releasing people from bondage but also ensures their overall welfare by transforming the world the freed people will live in. At the same time, the concept of integral transformation includes liberation. Integral transformation is inclusive as well as comprehensive, since it covers all aspects that impinge on human existence—social, religious, economic, political, and so on.

The word *liberation* is limited, since it leaves open the possibility that the powers and structures that held people in bondage will remain intact and retain their potential to oppress. On the contrary, the theology of integral transformation aims to liberate the oppressed and also transform the oppressive structures to enhance life permanently. A

---

3  J. Jayakiran Sebastian, "'Can We Now Bypass That Truth?'—Interrogating the Methodology of Dalit Theology," *Transformation* 25, nos. 2/3 (2008): 89.

4  Matous Holeka, "Reading the Bible in Various Streams of Liberation Theology: Latin American Theology, South African Black Theology and Indian Dalit Theology," *Communio Viatorium* 56, no. 2 (2014): 169–96.

theology aimed at integral transformation is not limited to any specific form or cause of suffering or any particular segment of the population. The goal of this approach is not just liberating individuals alone, but it leads them to build communities that govern their lives in love, forgiveness, and mutual help.

The theology of integral transformation follows the example of Jesus and his apostles. Jesus rejected the dominant ideology of his times with a goal to transform society. The power centers in the first century colluded to eliminate Jesus because his teachings threatened their very existence. He critiqued the religion and ideology of the time. Michael C. Elliott opines, "The most threatening thing about Jesus was that he was calling for a complete, one is tempted to say Utopian, reconstruction of the social, political and economic orders."[5]

A theology of integral transformation aims to make society more just, equitable, and harmonious; in other words, it aims to make the world as God intended it to be or like the kingdom of God that Jesus came to establish. The kingdom of God comes into existence gradually as the members of the kingdom extend their claim over all systems and structures to transform them. It is not replacing one system with another. As Elliott puts it, "The development of the Kingdom depends not upon the sudden overthrowal of one set of social, political and economic structures and their replacement by another, but on the members of the Kingdom gradually extending its claims over all systems and structures, transforming them in that process."[6]

The book falls into two parts. In the first part, I venture to explore the various aspects of Dalit liberation theology. For novices, this will be a simpler introduction, and experts may call it a critique—it is both at the same time. In the following chapters, I take a closer look at the methodologies and themes that Dalit theology has presented to us over the years. Dalit theology has to do with the Dalit reality, so I have examined various aspects of the Dalit reality in India. Furthermore, I have attempted to provide an overview of theological reflections on Dalits before the advent of this movement.

The second part uses the wisdom gathered from this assessment of Dalit theology over the last four decades to lay out some proposals for

---

5 Michael C. Elliott, *Freedom, Justice and Christian Counter-Culture* (Philadelphia: Trinity Press International, 1990), 38–39.
6 Elliott, 117.

the way forward. However, some retrospection is important in this project, so I have presented two case studies where the Christian witness in India has attempted to confront evils in society and the church. I argue that the nature, structure, and mission of the church in India must be rearticulated. This rearticulation must highlight the primacy of its mission of transformation. Besides making a case for a new ecclesiology, I also suggest that theology should reincarnate itself as public theology to address public affairs that impinge on human lives, particularly those of the subalterns. Only then can integral transformation be realized.

Finally, I must admit that I cannot call myself a Dalit theologian with any degree of confidence. But the origin of Dalit theology and my academic career happened simultaneously in time and space. Dalit liberation theology was happening all around me throughout my journey as a student of theology and teacher. I just could not ignore it. Some of the best scholars who have contributed to Dalit theology are my friends and colleagues; I have been in conversation with many of them while writing this book. Despite my indirect association with this academic discipline, my apparent dissociation gives me a special advantage of being more objective than many others who are immersed in it.

# PART I

## THE WAY IT IS

# 1

# CONTOURS OF DALIT THEOLOGY

Let us not seek to satisfy our thirst for freedom by drinking from
the cup of bitterness and hatred.

—Martin Luther King Jr.

## Birth and Growth

Dalit theology owes its origin to the speech Arvind P. Nirmal made at
the valedictory function of the Carey Society at the United Theological
College in 1983. In that speech, he outlined the need for and scope of
what he then called "Shudra Theology."[1] However, Nirmal replaced the
word *Shudra* with *Dalit* when he published the revised version of his
paper. The speech and its subsequent publication for a wider audience
marked the birth of modern Dalit theology. It launched a movement that
has inspired a steady stream of hermeneutical and theological works for
the last four decades.

There are at least three interrelated facets of Dalit theology that are
important for a proper understanding of what Dalit theology is and what
it is trying to achieve. Briefly put, Dalit theology is contextual, counter,
and liberational.

---

1 *Shudra*, also spelled *Soodra*, is the lowest caste in the traditional four-caste system of social organization in ancient India.

## The Contextual Nature of Theology

Christian theology has always been contextual. As José Miguez Bonino puts it, "Theology has always been contextual: implicitly or explicitly, consciously or unconsciously, deliberately or against the will of the theologian."[2] However, in the case of theologies that claim to be contextual, being relevant to the context is a conscious decision on the part of the theologian.

Though all theologies are contextual, the contextual theologies of the West and the so-called developing countries—the Global South—are different. Contextual theologies could be those of the dominant groups to serve their interests or those of the subalterns based on their experiences. Along with most theologies emerging from the Global South, Dalit theology belongs to the latter group. It is contextual because it is focusing not on the universal human experience but on human experience(s) specific to context—namely, the suffering of the Dalits in India.

Social realities are more important than philosophical reasoning for Dalit theology. Nirmal affirms that Dalit theology has moved from the "philosophical-propositional character of classical theologies."[3] Thus it is not philosophy but sociology that informs Dalit theology. Moreover, Nirmal argues that Dalit theology is rooted not in revelation but in the realities of the lives of the Dalits, their suffering. Other Dalit theologians, such as M. E. Prabhakar, follow suit; as Prabhakar says, "We understand the dalit condition neither purely spiritually nor exclusively materialistically, but existentially and dialectically at the same time."[4]

However, it is a paradox that like all contextual theologies in the Global South, Dalit theology also has a layer of Western forms of thought and influence. As John Parratt points out, contextual theologies in the Global South were possible because of the Western form of thinking and education that colonialism brought.[5]

2 José Miguez Bonino, "Latin America," in Parratt, *Introduction to Third World Theologies*, 31.

3 A. P. Nirmal, "Doing Theology from a Dalit Perspective," in *A Reader in Dalit Theology*, ed. Arvind P. Nirmal (Madras, India: Gurukul Lutheran Theological College, 1990), 140.

4 M. E. Prabhakar, "The Search for a Dalit Theology," in Nirmal, *Reader in Dalit Theology*, 44.

5 John Parratt, introduction to Parratt, *Introduction to Third World Theologies*, 11–25.

## Liberation Theology

Dalit theology is determined to liberate Dalits from their predicament, as the early founders declared that Dalit theology engages with the reality of the human experience of discrimination, subjugation, and violence. Nirmal and the Dalit theologians who followed him affirm that the goal of Dalit theology is Dalit liberation from their pathos.[6]

However, Dalit theology is a liberation theology that is unique in many ways. First, Dalit theology is unique in its vision of liberation, which is "authentically Indian."[7] Both traditional Indian Christian theology and the theologies of the Global South failed to include the Dalit condition in their agendas.[8] At least some liberation theologians from other contexts duly recognize this reality. For example, Black theologian James H. Cone admits that one "weakness" of his work is "the failure to link the African-American struggle for liberation in the United States with similar struggles in the Third World."[9] This is the gap that Dalit theology set out to fill.

Second, besides being authentically Indian, the nature and cause of the oppression it addresses are unique. K. W. Christopher rightly observes that "while Dalit theology is to some extent inspired by Latin American liberation theology, it replaces the latter's emphasis on economics with caste."[10] Liberation theology addressed the concerns of those who were of a lower economic class. However, caste is radically different from class. While a person can migrate to a higher class if conditions are feasible, a person of low-caste origin cannot erase the social stigma even by moving up to a higher economic class. Caste is something that a person is by birth, and that stigma sticks lifelong.

Third, Dalit theology is also unique in that at least initially, it envisioned active protests to achieve liberation. Its pioneers envisaged not only theological reflection on Dalit suffering but action as well. As Nirmal says, "Our *pathos* should give birth to our protest—a very loud

---

6  Arvind P. Nirmal, "Towards a Christian Dalit Theology," in Nirmal, *Reader in Dalit Theology*, 53–70.

7  Nirmal, 57.

8  Nirmal, 57.

9  James H. Cone, *Black Theology and Black Power* (Maryknoll, NY: Orbis, 2018), xxx.

10  K. W. Christopher, "Between Two Worlds: The Predicament of Dalit Christians in Bama's Works," *Journal of Commonwealth Literature* 47, no. 1 (March 1, 2012): 18.

protest. Our protest should be so loud that the walls of Brahmanism should come tumbling down. A Christian Dalit theology will be theology full of *pathos*, but not a passive theology."[11]

Fourth, Dalit theologians also argue that not only protest but resistance is important in the case of Dalit liberation. Sathianathan Clarke sees an interconnection between resistance and liberation. Resistance is required to avoid co-option by the dominant communities and their discourses. However, liberation is that link that connects all subjugated communities. Since liberation first requires resistance, he conceives of resistance as part of the trajectory that leads to liberation.[12]

Unlike some other liberation theologies of the Global South, Dalit theology has a narrow focus on socioeconomic conditions. For example, liberation theology in Africa has a wider scope, as Diane Stinton points out. Stinton cites Charles Nyamiti to say that liberation theology in independent Africa endeavors to integrate the theme of liberation into the rest of Africa's cultural background: "Liberation is not confined to modern socio-economic and political levels but includes emancipation from other forms of oppression such as disease, poverty, hunger, ignorance, and the subjugation of women."[13] Dalit theology, by contrast, is fixated on the social and economic disadvantages, ignoring other aspects of the Dalits' pain. For example, among many other things, the total sidelining of Dalit culture and language makes the Dalits irrelevant in the Indian scenario.

## Countertheology

Another important aspect of Dalit theology is that it is a countertheology. It is counter to the so-called Brahmanical approach in Christian theology. It aims to use Dalit categories of thought and to give expression to the Dalit experience of God. Dalit theology aspires to express what

11 Nirmal, "Towards a Christian Dalit Theology," 62.

12 Sathianathan Clarke, "Dalit Theology: An Introductory and Interpretive Theological Exposition," in *Dalit Theology in the Twenty-First Century: Discordant Voices, Discerning Pathways*, ed. Sathianathan Clarke, Manchala Deenabandhu, and Philip Peacock (New Delhi: Oxford University Press, 2010), 23.

13 Charles Nyamiti, "Contemporary African Christologies: Assessment and Practical Suggestions," in *Paths of African Theology*, ed. Rosino Gibellini (Maryknoll, NY: Orbis, 1994), 66, cited by Diane Stinton, "Africa, East and West," in Parratt, *Introduction to Third World Theologies*, 115.

Dalits think of the divine in their own modes of expression. For this matter, Dalit theology hoped to follow the principle of exclusion, because exclusion would give them the freedom and the leeway to be on their own and not controlled by others. Dalit theology aspired to be a theology of aspiration, self-narration, and alternative discourse.

As a countertheology, Dalit theology envisions itself as methodologically exclusive. It proposes to use its own methods instead of using existing hermeneutical methods, especially those rooted in the Brahmanical traditions. Clarke thinks that methodological exclusion creates room for creativity and "self-reflectivity."[14] The ideal of self-reflectivity would also imply a rejection of the patronizing theologies made by others on their behalf. It would be a theology of the people. So, Nirmal says, "a search and expression of identity therefore characterizes all liberation theologies and peoples' theologies."[15] Dalit theology thus longs to bring about a revolution in hermeneutics in the Indian theological tradition.

Though Clarke endorses the idea that Dalit theology will enable the Dalits to reflect on themselves, he is also critical of Dalit theology as an exclusive countertheology. If it is purely a countertheology, Dalit theology will be merely reactionary, without anything new to contribute: "While this resistive and oppositional tack must not be undervalued, one must be careful not to construct Dalit theology as essentially characterized by the prefix 'counter.' After all, Dalit theology cannot be captured as a systematic and significant reaction to another primordial theological discourse that is accepted as a given."[16]

Scholars like Clarke also express that countertheology will only promote an unhealthy "Self-Other dichotomy."[17]

## Dalit Theology and Its Siblings

As a contextual theology, Dalit theology follows in the footsteps of movements of similar strains that emerged years ago. Other contextual theologies that precede Dalit theology—namely, the Black theology movement in North America, Minjung theology in South Korea, and the liberation

---

14  Clarke, "Dalit Theology," 28.
15  Nirmal, "Doing Theology," 143, cited in Clarke, "Dalit Theology," 28.
16  Clarke, "Dalit Theology," 27.
17  Clarke, 27.

theology movement in Latin America and other countries—provided the template for Dalit theology, on which it is heavily dependent.

Black theology, which emerged in North America in the 1970s, is an older sibling with whom Dalit theology shares its DNA. Dalit theology and Black theology share many features. First, both address very similar contextual realities—namely, discrimination based on one's identity. In the case of Black theology, it is racial discrimination, while in the case of Dalit theology, the discrimination is based on caste. In both cases, such discrimination has led to social, economic, and political disadvantages.

But there are obvious differences between Black theology and Dalit theology. Black theology is inspired by the US civil rights movement and the Black Power movement. In the introduction of the 1989 edition of *Black Theology and Black Power*, James Cone writes that his book is the product of "Civil Rights and Black Power movements in America during the 1960s, reflecting both their strengths and weaknesses."[18] As we will see later in this work, Dalit theology doesn't have such a heritage; it is a theology in isolation.

Black theology, like Latin American liberation theology, addressed the white Christian conscience that produced the Black condition. A Christian conscience did not produce the Dalit predicament, so Dalit theology does not have to address it. It is difficult to find Christian theologians rationalizing caste-based oppression, even though they might have accommodated it. This is contrary to US slavery, where a lot of theology was produced to justify and perpetuate oppression. We will review this aspect of Dalit theology in detail later in this work.

Minjung theology is another movement that could be called a sibling of Dalit theology. The social and economic injustices suffered by the common people had already become the concern of Christian theology in South Korea in the form of Minjung theology around the 1970s. As Vedran Golijanin rightly points out, Minjung theology originated not in the academies but at the grassroots level as ordinary people began to reject theologies that suggested that they subject themselves to their persecutors.[19] According to A. Sung Park, academics who stood against the oppression and subsequently lost their jobs in the universities articulated

---

18  Cone, *Black Theology and Black Power*, xxv.
19  Vedran Golijanin, "Jesus Christ and the Minjung in Korean Liberation Theology," *Godišnjak, Journal of Faculty of Orthodox Theology* 2, no. 12 (2013): 51–72.

Minjung theology for the ordinary people.[20] It was not empathetic or sympathetic epistemology but knowledge that emerged from a genuine firsthand experience of pathos that resulted in Minjung theology.

In contrast, real Dalits were not the subjects of Dalit theology; rather, those who were educated either in the West or in Western modes of thought produced Dalit theology. However, they do not seem to have realized the limitations Cone honestly admits. Cone sees that his Western education has influenced his theology, and that is one of the limitations of his work *Black Theology and Black Power*.

Liberation theology in Latin America also has a similar bottom-up approach that Dalit theology cannot claim. Latin American liberation theology emerged from and propagated through the base communities. Dalit theology, unlike all the contextual and liberation theologies that share the same DNA, fails in this aspect.

## Objects of Dalit Theology

One of the major discussions in the early stages of its development was regarding the subjects and objects of Dalit theology.

In the early days, it seems that Dalit theology assumed that its objects were Dalit converts to Christianity. This is how Dalit theology was done in its early years. In Nirmal's words, Dalit theology recognizes the exodus experience of Christian Dalits. The experience of Christian Dalits is different from that of other Dalits. He says, "Let Christian dalits also affirm their own exodus experience. What I mean is that as we should be aware of our historical dalit consciousness, so we should also be aware of our present Christian consciousness, so we are not just dalits, we are Christian dalits. Something has happened to us. Our status has changed."[21]

In order to counter this fixation on Dalit Christians, Dhyanchand Carr proposes to widen the scope of Dalit theology to include non-Christian Dalits. He says, "Dalit theology is not concerned with Christian Dalits but with all dalits of India."[22]

---

20  A. Sung Park, "Minjung Theology: A Korean Contextual Theology," *Indian Journal of Theology* 33 (1984): 1–11.

21  Arvind P. Nirmal, "A Dialogue with Dalit Literature," in *Towards a Dalit Theology*, ed. M. E. Prabhakar (New Delhi: ISPCK, 1988), 80, cited in Clarke, "Dalit Theology," 29.

22  Dhyanchand Carr, "Dalit Theology Is Biblical and It Makes the Gospel Relevant," in Nirmal, *Reader in Dalit Theology*, 72.

Nirmal seems to have revised his approach later to include both Christian and non-Christian Dalits in his envisioning of Dalit theology. According to him, the common struggle of the Dalits—Christian and non-Christian—will shape Dalit theology. He says that in Dalit theology, "the primacy of the term 'dalit' will have to be conceded as against the primacy of the term 'Christian' in the dominant theological primary."[23] He later clarified, "It is the common dalit experience of Christian dalits along with other dalits that will shape a Christian dalit theology."[24] It seems that over the four decades of Dalit theology's life, there is still no clarity in this regard; this confusion as to whom Dalit theology addresses remains.

## Subjects of Dalit Theology

Since it has to do with Dalit experience and the ways of knowing that experience of pathos (suffering), discussions of the subjects of Dalit theology also have an important place. James Massey, a stalwart in Dalit theology, proposes that Dalits should have the right to be the subject of their theology.[25] Clarke joins with Massey, saying that Dalit theology is aspirational, and Dalits must have the privilege of "construing their own versions of God-world-human that would be profoundly biblical, genuinely theological, intensely experiential, and truly liberational."[26] However, neither Massey, nor Clarke, nor others who advocate that Dalits should be the primary subjects of Dalit theology exclude others as Prabhakar has. He limits the scope of Dalit theology to a "theology of the dalits by the dalits for the dalits."[27]

Prabhakar's exclusion of non-Dalits from Dalit theology is highly idealistic. Though most Dalit theology is produced by theologians of Dalit origin, their Dalit experience has been secondary. For example, Nirmal, the godfather of Dalit theology, was distanced from the Dalit experience by at least two generations.

Nirmal had objective knowledge of Dalit experience, especially that of the Christian Dalits. Though he was positioned socially and physically

---

23  Nirmal, "Towards a Christian Dalit Theology," 59.

24  Nirmal, 59.

25  See James Massey, *Towards Dalit Hermeneutics: Rereading the Text, the History and the Literature* (New Delhi: ISPCK, 1994), 106.

26  Clarke, "Dalit Theology," 29.

27  Prabhakar, "Search for a Dalit Theology," 47.

away from the Dalit sufferings that his grandfather's generation had gone through, he knew what it was to be a Dalit in India through his pastoral experiences in the Church of North India. This objective rather than the subjective experience of Dalit pathos is what Nirmal proposed should be used as the hermeneutical key to Dalit theology.

His academic prowess, his objective experience of the Dalit pathos, and the memory of his grandparents' Dalit experience of discrimination made Nirmal identify three potential subjects of Dalit theology. Nirmal argues that though authentic Dalit theology can be done only by Dalits, others can also do Dalit theology from two other levels of knowing Dalit pathos.

Nirmal proposes three modes of knowledge—pathetic, empathetic, and sympathetic.[28] Pathetic knowledge is the firsthand knowledge of one's own experience. Empathetic knowledge is available to those who can empathize with those who suffer.[29] The third mode of knowledge is sympathetic knowledge, which is possible for those who, though they are not Dalits, can identify with the Dalit pathos and want to alleviate Dalit suffering. As Nirmal says, "To them belongs the sympathetic knowing. The firsthand experience of dalit pathos is not theirs, but they want to sympathize with the dalits."[30] Though Nirmal proposed three approaches to Dalit theology, which include non-Dalits, he still longed for Dalit theology to be largely empathetic, or done by those with an authentic first-hand experience of Dalit pathos.[31]

Nirmal's classification of Dalit theology reflects an approach similar to the one John C. B. Webster proposes. It is difficult to say who influenced whom. Webster imagines Dalit theology, which he called the theology of the depressed classes, as *about* them, *for* them, and *by* them.[32]

Webster thus opens up the possibility of Dalit theology done by non-Dalits as well. Recognizing the possibility of "theology *about* the Depressed classes or theological reflection upon the Christian responsibility to the Depressed Classes," he extends the enterprise to all those

---

28  Nirmal, "Doing Theology," 142.
29  Nirmal, 142.
30  Nirmal, 142.
31  Nirmal, "Towards a Christian Dalit Theology," 58.
32  For reasons known only to him, Webster used the expression "depressed classes" for Dalits in his writings.

who have objective knowledge of the Dalits.[33] Webster's second definition of Dalit theology also allows any non-Dalits to write Dalit theology. In his own words, it is a "theology *for* the Depressed Classes, or the theology of the message addressed to them and to which they seemed to be responding."[34] So anyone who is concerned about the Dalits could do theology addressed to them. Third, Webster recognizes the source of Dalit theology is Dalits themselves. He writes, "Theology *from* the Depressed Classes, that is the theology which they themselves have held or produced."[35]

Both Nirmal and Webster propose that Dalit theology should be a project that includes Dalits and non-Dalits as its subjects. However, Clarke agrees with Nirmal's proposition, as he suggests that "the intention of invoking theological inclusiveness of Dalit theology is to allow for Christian communitarian interrelatedness in the task of overcoming suffering for Dalits and all those who suffer the effects of oppression. Other communities can participate in doing Dalit theology but must recognize their respective distance and respectful relatedness to the distinctiveness of Dalit pain-pathos."[36]

To further the scope of the Dalit theological enterprise, Clarke refines the pathos by imagining it in three concentric circles of varying intensity. Clarke visualizes three modes of knowledge in concentric circles with lesser pathos as we move out from the center (pathetic) to the outermost (sympathetic). He uses the metaphor of the body feeling the pain of a blow—the point that takes the blow feels intense pain, but as the pain reverberates through the body, it becomes less at the outer extremities.[37]

Clarke's definition of Dalit theology reflects the reality of the Dalit theological enterprise of the times. He defines Dalit theology as follows: "Dalit theology, thus, as a discourse about God intricately related to the world and human beings, assumes the freedom and integrity for Dalits to be subjects. To be subject only to God also implies not to be subjected by other human beings."[38] Clarke's understanding of Dalit theology has to do with what God has done, is doing, and has to do in the lives of the

---

33  John C. B. Webster, "From Indian Church to Indian Theology: An Attempt at Theological Construction," in Nirmal, *Reader in Dalit Theology*, 106.

34  Webster, 106.

35  Webster, 106.

36  Clarke, "Dalit Theology," 22.

37  Clarke, 22.

38  Clarke, 24.

Dalits. This theological enterprise presumes the freedom and integrity of the Dalits to be the sole subjects of their own experience. Clarke thus affirms that Dalit theology assumes the right of Dalits to be subjects but doesn't seem to deny those who are non-Dalits by either race or experience from being participants in the Dalit theological enterprise. Sympathetic and empathetic involvement in the Dalit theological enterprise is still possible.

Nirmal, Webster, and later Clarke widened the scope of who could do Dalit theology. This is one of the reasons Dalit liberation theology became a thriving academic discipline, through wider participation. At the same time, this could also be the reason real Dalits without academic skills became nonparticipants in this movement for them, about them, and proposed to be by them.

These discussions on the objects and subjects of Dalit theology are important. However, the largely ignored elephant in the room is, Whom should Dalit theology address? Should Dalit theology address Dalits who suffer or those people and systems that cause their suffering? Dalit theology failed to identify that such an issue even exists.

Another important question that we should ask with the benefit of hindsight is, Did real Dalits with pathetic epistemology create Dalit theology? The answer is a qualified no. Dalit theology was made mostly by people with Western-style theological educations whose tools were anything other than typically Dalit. A survey of Dalit theological writings shows that all of it is produced by academically competent people who have moved away from the grassroots Dalit realities for generations. Thus the segment that we can imagine as Dalit theology by authentic Dalits who have an empathetic knowledge of Dalit pathos is waiting to be made. However, Dalit theology has thrived as a discipline through the participation of scholars of Dalit origin and non-Dalits.

## Conclusion

We have explored the main contours of Dalit theology, which I would like to summarize here before venturing further. Dalit theology is unique in many ways, since it is the only liberation theology of the Indian subcontinent. As a contextual theology, it has caused Indian theologians to be rooted in their own context instead of wandering in the wider landscape of theology, exploring philosophical themes. This contextual awareness led them to reflect on the suffering of the Dalits in India and their liberation. This act of rooting in the context has in fact liberated theological reflection from merely echoing Western traditions alien to the theologians and their clients as well.

This contextual theology, with its explicit objective of liberation, was unhappy with the way theology was done by high-caste converts in the Indian church, so it positioned itself as a countertheology opposed to the Brahmanical interpretation of the Christian faith. However, it was not merely reactionary; rather, Dalit theologians hoped that as a countertheology, it would enable the Dalits to voice their aspirations and experiences in their own way and in their own modes.

Nevertheless, Dalit theology is not clear about for whom the theology is made. It remains to be answered if the scope of Dalit theology is limited to Dalits in the Christian churches or Dalits in general in society. It is also not clear if the suffering that they try to address is merely caste inflicted or if wider issues of the suffering masses are within the scope. The pain of the Dalits is not self-created; they are victims of powerful people, social forces, and power structures. But as Keith Hebden points out, Dalit theology lacks a "theology of powers."[39]

Nirmal and Webster, followed by Clarke, widened the scope of Dalit theology by allowing suffering Dalits and all those who are engaged and interested in their plight to join. This, however, resulted in making it more academic than participatory.

After four decades of its existence amid the voices of its enthusiasts, voices of discontentment are also emerging in the Dalit theology movement. Fellow travelers in the movement have begun to raise questions that beg for answers. For example, after assessing the performance of Dalit theology over three decades, Peniel Rajkumar declares that the practical efficacy of Dalit theology is nil. He writes, "This incompatibility in my opinion is symptomatic of the practical inefficacy of Dalit theology. Dalit theology does not seem to have significantly influenced the social practice of the Indian Church."[40] In a similar way, Dalit feminist theologian Surekha Nelavala remarks that "even though Dalit theology is, without question, a people-centered theological phenomenon, it has not reached out to the masses and thus has not yet proven to be effective

---

39  Keith Hebden, *Dalit Theology and Christian Anarchism*, New Critical Thinking in Religion, Theology, and Biblical Studies (Farnham, UK: Ashgate, 2011), 137.
40  Peniel Rajkumar, *Dalit Theology and Dalit Liberation: Problems, Paradigms and Possibilities* (London: Routledge, 2016), 1.

in its praxis objective."[41] Are these the voices of the dispirited sailors who longed to forge ahead toward new horizons but have woken up to find that the ship has entered the doldrums? Or are we trying to keep something afloat even though it has lost steam? We should avoid jumping to quick judgments before exploring other aspects of Dalit theology.

---

41  Surekha Nelavala, "Martin Luther's Concept of Sola Scriptura and Its Impact on the Masses: A Dalit Model for Praxis-Nexus," *Seminary Ridge Review; Gettysburg* 15, no. 2 (Spring 2013): 68.

# 2

# METHODOLOGIES
# AND THEMES

Research is a two-way process, search for what you have gained and what you have to lose; what you have lost and what you have to gain.

—P. S. Jagadeesh Kumar

Dalit theology emerged declaring a revolution of hermeneutics in Indian theology. So the scrutiny of various aspects of Dalit theology should begin with the hermeneutical methods that Dalit theologians have employed over the past four decades.

## The Vision of Dalit Hermeneutics

One of the most enviable aspects of Dalit theology is that it has a radical vision of a hermeneutics that is unique and liberative. Dalit hermeneutics aims to give Dalits a voice in Indian theology in opposition to prevailing Brahmanical voices. Dalits have always outnumbered high-caste converts to Christianity in India. However, lack of literacy and a comparatively lower level of education have stifled their voices in the Indian church. On the contrary, the voices of the minority of high-caste converts who were more educated and more articulate dominated the scene. Arvind P. Nirmal and other Dalit theologians who shadowed him argue that it is time for the voice of the Dalits to be heard in the Indian theological scenario.

As Clarke points out, the purpose of Dalit theology is "to scuttle the unproblematic unitary march of Indian Christian theology towards possible Brahmanic captivity."[1] Nirmal's proposal for a new way of imagining Indian Christian theology arose in this context.[2] Indian Christian theology—allegedly Brahmanical—was conceptually devoid of contextual realities, especially Dalit suffering.[3] As Christopher says, Dalit theology "is opposed to mainstream Indian Christian theology that interprets Christianity in Brahmanical terms."[4]

Though it is true that converts from high castes dominated the scene, imagining a Brahmanical conspiracy against the Dalits or Dalit Christians is unfounded. Indian Christian theology before Dalit theology is characterized by its age. All the Indian theologians critiqued by Dalit theologians lived and worked in a period predating the global shift in theological thinking from universal, timeless concepts to contextual and specific issues and struggles of peoples. They should be forgiven because they represented the spirit of their age—the zeitgeist.

Further, attaching a caste tone to conventional Indian Christian theology is also wrong. The so-called Brahmanical approach to the Christian Bible did not create, justify, or promulgate the Dalit predicament, though it ignored the social reality of the oppressed along with all other human realities.

Though Dalit theology is conceived of as a countertheology, it has not countered any Brahmanical approaches explicitly. On the contrary, it has explored alternate approaches, often influenced by the prevalent trends in the wider academy. A closer look at the participants, methodology, and assumptions of Dalit hermeneutics seems to indicate that Dalit hermeneutics has not broken any new ground in favor of the Dalits. Dalit theologians have not brought any unique Dalit categories of thought to theological reasoning in India, though the Dalits have their own epistemology, experience, and modes of expression to create rich

---

1 Clarke, "Dalit Theology," 35.
2 Nirmal, "Towards a Christian Dalit Theology," 55.
3 Before Dalit theology made its appearance, Indian Christian theology was dominated by high-caste converts to Christianity such as Brahmabandhav Upadhyay (1861–1907), Sadhu Sunder Singh (1889–death unknown), Nehemiah Gore (1825–95), H. A. Krishna Pillai (1827–1900), Narayan Vaman Tilak (1861–1919), A. J. Appasamy (1891–1975), P. Chenchiah (1886–1959), and V. Chakkarai (1880–1958).
4 Christopher, "Between Two Worlds," 18.

Dalit theological reflection.[5] These have been overlooked in favor of movements in biblical hermeneutics.

## Methodologies

A cursory survey of literature in Dalit theology leads one to conclude that the historical-grammatical method of biblical interpretation and reader-centered approaches have been the most popular methods employed by Dalit theologians. Wherever Dalit theologians deviate from a literal reading of the Bible, they resort to reader-centered approaches. Dalit theologians have found this approach convenient for their purposes, since it allows readers shaped by various factors, such as their social location, cultural influences, economic status, or political inclinations, to bring meaning to the text. In practice, most of Dalit hermeneutics were rather reading the Bible from Dalit perspectives, particularly from the perspective of their suffering.

### Pathos: The Master Key

Nirmal proposed that Dalit suffering or pathos should be the hermeneutical key to Dalit theology, because knowing is not through revelation or through the combination of faith and reason. Dalit theology, like other liberation theologies, affirms "the basic unity between theory and practice and thought and action." Nirmal further asserts that for a Dalit theology, "pain or Pathos is the beginning of knowledge."[6] Pathos remains the sole and dominant hermeneutical key to Dalit theology. This suggests that Dalit theology presumes Dalits are in a perpetual condition of suffering that needs to be addressed.

The Dalit pathos that the Dalit theologians addressed was limited to their socioeconomic conditions. Dalit theology overemphasizes physical and economic oppression, ignoring the psychological and spiritual oppression of the Dalits. Paul Bubash observes that "what these people suffer from most is a psychological and spiritual oppression that comes with the identity of being a non-person. In the Dalit experience, economic

---

5   For the contributions that Dalits and tribals have made to culture, language, industry, and so on, see Kancha Ilaiah, *Post-Hindu India: A Discourse on Dalit-Bahujann, Socio-spiritual and Scientific Revolution* (New Delhi: Sage, 2009).

6   Nirmal, "Doing Theology," 141.

poverty and social ostracisation only serve to reinforce the belief that one is rejected by God."[7]

This focus on suffering is well attested. For example, even after three decades of Dalit theology, theologians like Clarke have continued to affirm that "Dalit theology is founded on the 'pathetic' experience of specific Dalit communities, filtered through the inspirational person and work of Jesus Christ, and entwined into the lives of the oppressed peoples in India with the objective of funding and finding life in all its fullness for all human beings."[8]

However, reflecting on this preoccupation with Dalit pathos, Bonita Aleaz advocates for a widening of the concerns of Dalit theology. She says, "It is not suffering, Dalit pathos alone but also their experience of struggle to overcome suffering and their determination to risk themselves for the sake of liberation and justice that now needs to be considered as the subject matter of theological reflection."[9]

Furthermore, for most Dalit theologians, the pathos they have employed as the hermeneutical key was more imagined than experienced. Prasuna Gnana Nelavala, a Dalit feminist theologian, honestly admits this limitation, pointing out that there exists a distance between academic discourse and the Dalits. She says, "I admit that grass root Dalit women are often unfamiliar with the way I write and reflect and that sometimes they are not even aware of their own struggles. I confess that a certain distance exists between academic theology and the daily life of Dalit women."[10]

This is true in the case of not only Dalit women but Dalit men as well. Contemporary Dalit theologians, though they seem to condemn Western theological disciplines, have been trained in Western theological institutions and follow Western academic traditions. Their works have also been published by academic publishers in the West. This leads us to conclude that the previous four decades of Dalit theology were ones of sympathetic or empathetic engagements mostly and were seldom pathetic. It was mostly not *by* the Dalits but *about* the Dalits and *for* the

---

7  Paul Bubash, "Dalit Theology and Spiritual Oppression: A Call to Holiness in a Universal Church," *Journal of Theta Alpha Kappa* 38, no. 2 (September 2014): 44.

8  Clarke, "Dalit Theology," 19.

9  Bonita Aleaz, "Expressions of Dalit Christian Identity," *Contemporary Voice of Dalit* 5, no. 1 (January 1, 2012): 33.

10  Prasuna Gnana Nelavala, "Caste Branding, Bleeding Body, Building Dalit Womanhood. Touchability of Jesus," in Clarke, Deenabandhu, and Peacock, *Dalit Theology*, 267.

Dalits by those who had already distanced themselves from the real Dalit experience socially and academically.

Though Dalit pathos still lingers as the dominant hermeneutical key, we should not ignore other methods proposed over the years even though they did not find wider acceptance.

### Pathos to Ethos

Dalit theology did attempt a shift in hermeneutical approaches. We find a lone voice in Peniel Rajkumar, who made a significant move forward in Dalit hermeneutics by proposing the Dalithos (Dalit + ethos) reading. He revolted, stating that pathos is not the only key that can be employed in Dalit hermeneutics, but the ethos of the Dalits is also a valid hermeneutical key.[11] A Dalithos reading requires a knowledge of the ethos of the Dalits documented in sociological, anthropological, and cultural studies.[12] Rajkumar's work is a good example of how the Dalit ethos can be woven into a reading of biblical texts. However, even to this day, Rajkumar remains the lone voice in Dalithos reading. Dalit hermeneutics is still stuck at Dalit pathos.

### Hermeneutics of Resistance: Christ as Drum

Another significant voice in Dalit hermeneutics is that of Sathianathan Clarke.[13] He had a long ministry experience among the Paraiyars in Tamil Nadu, and his contribution to Dalit hermeneutics is influenced by his engagement with this community. He argues that the drum beating of the Paraiyars is an act of mediation with the divine and a resistance to the powers, particularly of the caste Hindus who dominate them. In his own words, "The drum, no doubt, symbolizes the resistive and emancipatory power of the Divine as the Paraiyar confront, contest and combat the demonizing and colonizing proclivities of the caste communities."[14] He suggests that since the drum is not limited to the Paraiyar community, it has a universal appeal among the Dalits of South India. He developed his

---

11 Peniel Jesudason Rufus Rajkumar, "A Dalithos Reading of a Markan Exorcism: Mark 5:1–20," *Expository Times* 118, no. 9 (June 1, 2007): 428.

12 Rajkumar.

13 Sathianathan Clarke, *Dalits and Christianity: Subaltern Religion and Liberation Theology in India* (New Delhi: Oxford University Press, 1998).

14 Clarke, 166.

Christology around the mediation of Christ and the power of resistance, which led him to propose that a hermeneutics of resistance must be built around the symbol of the drum.

Clarke's contribution is ingenious because it points out the need to identify symbols of resistance that various Dalit communities other than the Paraiyars employ. But such explorations into the Dalit world of symbols seem to have ended with Clarke's contribution. New ground has yet to be broken.

### Hermeneutics of Affirmation: The Significance of the Dalit Body

While Clarke proposes a hermeneutics of resistance, Evangeline Anderson-Rajkumar's proposal could be termed a hermeneutics of affirmation. In her seminal article, Anderson-Rajkumar talks about how the Dalits' dark skin color is disdained in a society where fair skin is considered ideal.[15] She argues that contrary to scientific evidence that dark skin is the best protection against UV rays and so on, society still holds dark skin in contempt. Dark skin is also considered a symbol of impurity.[16] She contends that Dalit bodies should be used as tools of hermeneutics and theologizing: "Dalit hermeneutics always affirms in community and communitarian values. Body affirmation is at the centre of it all."[17] However, this proposal was also duly ignored and remains a voice in the wilderness.

## Themes in Dalit Theology

This survey of hermeneutical methods demands an examination of the themes Dalit theologians have explored. This will help us assess the liberative potential of Dalit theology.

---

15 Evangeline Anderson-Rajkumar, "Skin, Body and Blood: Explorations for Dalit Hermeneutics," *Religion and Society* 49, no. 2 (September 2004): 106–12.
16 Not all Dalits in India are dark skinned. However, Anderson-Rajkumar is situated in the southern part of India, where most of the Dalits who claim a Dravidian ancestry have dark skin. Dalits are not designated by their physical features like, for example, African Americans.
17 Anderson-Rajkumar, "Skin, Body and Blood," 119.

## A Nonviolent Dalit God

One of the noble goals of Dalit liberation theology is to free people from the fears that subjugate them. Dalit theology's conception of the divine is an important theme in this regard. Dalit theologians argue that the Dalits should conceive of God as a "Dalit God," to present an image of God that contradicts the conception promoted by their oppressors. Nirmal points out that the oppressors conceived of and promoted God as a violent judge who demands obedience and submission. He protests that "a non-dalit deity cannot be the god of dalits."[18] V. Devasahayam further elaborates that Dalits should understand God as a nonviolent God. The portrayal of God as a ruthless judge was convenient to exploit the Dalits and make them subservient. He observes, "God is imaged in the traditional formulations as the sovereign almighty and unmoved Mover. Moreover, God is conceived of as a ruthless judge, a heavenly Shylock demanding an eye for an eye."[19]

As a corollary, Dalit theologians hold that the image of Jesus that the New Testament presents would be more welcome. According to Devasahayam, Jesus "comes in weakness and humility and stands with those despised and suffering people."[20] This perception of God, contrary to the image of a violent God that was meant to impose fear on the Dalits and demanded their subjugation, is expressed in various ways. The image of God as a servant is one of those ways.

## God as Servant

Dalit theology is incarnational in its approach. It tries to conceive of God as someone who has come down to the level of humans to identify with them as a servant. This idea of God as a servant is compatible with the Dalit reality of years of servitude to high-caste employers and feudal lords. In one of his earliest writings, Nirmal reflects on God thus: "He is a servant God—a God who serves. Service has always been the privilege of Dalit communities in India. . . . Against this background the amazing

---

18  Clarke, "Dalit Theology," 25.

19  Clarke, 25.

20  V. Devasahayam, "The Nature of Dalit Theology as Counter Theology," in *Frontiers of Dalit Theology*, ed. V. Devasahayam (Delhi: ISPCK/Gurukul, 1997), 54, cited in Clarke, "Dalit Theology," 26.

claim of a Christian Dalit theology will be that the God of the dalits, the self-existent, the *svayambhu*, does not create others to do service work, but does servile work himself."[21]

Clarke affirms that this view of God as a servant helps Dalits imagine God in a way that is close to them and empowers them. He says it removes "the distance and aloofness of God from toiling people and bring[s] the Divine close to what was thought to be 'polluting' locations."[22]

Though he supports the identification of God with Dalits, Clarke is also critical of this view of God as a servant. He suggests that bringing God to their level as a servant deprives them of the possibility of imagining him as a God of power who can liberate them.[23]

Furthermore, the conception of God as a servant to the exclusion of his other traits is contrary to the Dalit experience and worldview. It is well known that the Dalit worldview deifies their human heroes rather than humanifies God. The existence of various cults among the Dalits and other subjugated communities in which they elevated their heroes to the level of objects of worship testifies that the Dalits cannot imagine the divine as one among them. The most evident example is Baba Saheb Ambedkar, the Dalit thinker and founder of neo-Buddhism, who is venerated by Dalits. Moreover, according to social historians like Badri Narayan, the Dalits have preserved folk songs and tales that deify local Dalit heroes, though they were later manipulated by politicians for their own advantages.[24]

One of the significant theological contributions of Dalit theologians is Christology. It is rather a corollary to the conceptions of God discussed earlier.

### Jesus the Suffering Servant

Nirmal modeled Jesus Christ as the suffering servant, and this has been a dominant theme of Dalit theology ever since. Kondasingu Jesurathnam elaborates that "Dalit Christology is deeply rooted in the suffering

21 Nirmal, "Towards a Christian Dalit Theology," 64.
22 Clarke, "Dalit Theology," 30.
23 Clarke, 30.
24 Badri Narayan, *Women Heroes and Dalit Assertion in North India: Culture, Identity and Politics* (New Delhi: Sage, 2006).

servant model of Jesus Christ, a perfect model for a suffering Dalit community in their daily lives."[25]

However, having surveyed Dalit Christologies that use the suffering servant model, Anderson H. M. Jeremiah concludes that this model is inadequate, since in this portrayal, Jesus is a meek Dalit, predestined to suffer.[26] Furthermore, Clarke concurs that this sole emphasis on the humanity of Jesus is inadequate for liberation. He suggests that the human and the divine aspects of Jesus Christ must be emphasized equally. There is an overemphasis on the humanity of Jesus. He says, "To empower the powerless and the afflicted, Indian Christian theology needs to recover both (a) the distinct social locatedness and the concrete social praxis of Jesus and (b) the tangible aspects of the cosmic potency of Jesus."[27] Furthermore, Jesurathnam agrees with Clarke, saying that the divine-human dimensions of Jesus Christ must both be preserved.[28]

### Jesus the Dalit

A corollary of the conception of Jesus as a suffering servant is the allied concept of Jesus as a Dalit. When portraying Jesus as a Dalit, Dalit theologians take it in the sense of weakness and powerlessness. Nirmal also sees Jesus Christ as a Dalit and his mission as for the Dalits.[29] For example, Nirmal identified the Dalit pathos with that of Jesus. This theme has reverberated throughout Dalit theology since its inception in various ways. For example, Prabhakar identifies Jesus as a Dalit in his incarnation. Prabhakar also rather arbitrarily suggests that Jesus is a Dalit because his blood was not pure.[30]

---

25  Kondasingu Jesurathnam, *Dalit Liberative Hermeneutics: Indian Christian Dalit Interpretation of Psalm 22* (New Delhi: ISPCK, 2010), 210.

26  Anderson H. M. Jeremiah, "Exploring New Facets of Dalit Christology: Critical Interaction with J. D. Crossan's Portrayal of Jesus," in Clarke, Deenabandhu, and Peacock, *Dalit Theology*, 150–67.

27  Sathianathan Clarke, "The Jesus of Nineteenth Century Indian Christian Theology: An Indian Inculturation with Continuing Problems and Prospects," *Studies in World Christianity* 5, no. 1 (1999): 43–44, cited in Jesurathnam, *Dalit Liberative Hermeneutics*, 171.

28  Jesurathnam, *Dalit Liberative Hermeneutics*, 171.

29  Nirmal, "Towards a Christian Dalit Theology," 65–69.

30  For a survey of this theme in Dalit theology, see Bubash, "Dalit Theology," 41–42.

There are dissenting voices among Dalit theologians in this regard too. For example, for Jesurathnam, the Dalitness of Jesus is not in what he was but in what he did. Jesurathnam states, "Jesus Christ is a Dalit because he manifested and displayed on the cross God's love for all humanity, in particular to the broken and oppressed, downtrodden and marginalized Dalits."[31] His comment seems to implicitly suggest that Jesus is Dalit in his willingness to sacrifice his life for the sake of others.

This notion of Dalit theology loudly echoes similar statements by other liberation theologies—that Jesus is Black or Jesus is Minjung. Dalit theology's indebtedness to liberation theologies of other contexts is evident. But we should not ignore the differences. Though Black theologian James Cone argues that Jesus is Black, he does not mean that being Black, Jesus is powerless.[32] On the contrary, he identifies Jesus's Blackness with power. In this sense, Jesus as Black is more justifiable than Jesus as Dalit because Jesus is not a passive victim of his low origin or status in society. He stands in the traditions of prophets who were political dissenters and voices of liberation. Even his place of origin, Galilee, was one of political assertion and resurgence in the context of subjugation. Galilee was a place from which rebels arose to challenge oppression and subjugation.

Dalit Christology is selective in using biblical resources. Another important criticism of Dalit Christology is that it not only limits itself to the incarnated Christ of the Gospels but also largely ignores the Christ of the Epistles and especially of the book of Revelation, who is a liberator and vindicator.

We should not overlook the fact that the Christ who identifies with the Dalits as he becomes one of them in his humanity is also the *Christus Victor*, the one who has overcome the world's powers and death. Christology should not be terminated at the manger or the cross but should move beyond to the vision of the open grave and the lamb on the throne in heaven. Incarnational Christology alone could serve the purpose of Dalit liberation.

The Christ of the Epistles has conquered evil and empowered those who trust in him to conquer evil. The portrayal of Christ in the Epistles is the source from which the disciples of Jesus Christ drew power for their

31  Jesurathnam, *Dalit Liberative Hermeneutics*, 211.
32  Mary M. Veeneman, *Introducing Theological Method: A Survey of Contemporary Theologians and Approaches* (Grand Rapids, MI: Baker Academic, 2017), 136, Kindle.

liberative mission. Christ came to identify with humans to the extent of being a dying servant—that is one aspect of Christ. But though Jesus Christ identified with the suffering of humanity in his baptism and his death on the cross, he ascended to his Father's presence and sat on his right side (Phil 2:6–11). These two aspects must be held together.

Dalit theologians were so lost in the Jesus of the Synoptics that they ignored the fact that Christ subdued the powers of this world, which the Epistles proclaim loudly. The exalted Christ has authority over the authorities and systems of the world (Col 2:15). The Christ of the Apocalypse is the one who, in his meekness and majesty, has conquered the oppressors and vindicates the victims. He is the final victor. We should not lose sight of these themes by focusing narrowly on pathos; doing so makes Dalit Christology powerless.

Mainstream Dalit Christology has also come under the fire of Dalit feminist theologians who oppose the Christology of powerlessness. Evangeline Anderson argues that the birth of Jesus should be a point of discussion in womanist Christology. Intercaste births are a challenge to the caste system, which disciplines and punishes the violation of the lines they demarcate. Intercaste and interracial marriages threaten caste integrity. Anderson remarks that "as wombs become highly politicized space, it has to be affirmed simultaneously as the most subversive place to bring about change in the world."[33] She goes on to argue that in Christ's incarnation, God sidestepped "the patriarchalized, masculinized male."[34] Thus to "reread the purpose of Jesus being born of a virgin has definitely a new and a different scope in the rearticulation of Christology in context within a womanist framework and method."[35]

The argument that not a powerless, suffering Jesus but a Jesus of power should be the central theme of liberative Christology is further pointed out by Surekha Nelavala. She contends that it is not a suffering Dalit Jesus but an empowering Jesus who lends his voice to support the oppressed. Commenting on the anointing of Jesus at the house of Simon the Pharisee, she notes the patriarchal voice of Simon the Pharisee but also notes the stance of Jesus (Luke 7:36–50). While the Pharisee uses his privileged status to condemn the woman, Jesus uses his privileged

---

33  Evangeline Anderson, "Turning Bodies Inside Out: Contours of Womanist Theology," in Clarke, Deenabandhu, and Peacock, *Dalit Theology*, 211.

34  Anderson, 212.

35  Anderson, 212.

status to affirm the woman.[36] Nelavala perceives Jesus as antipatriarchal, profeminist, and pro–marginalized person.

Another dissenting voice to the popular Christologies that Dalit theologians have promoted comes from Bama. Roja Singh points out that Bama's Christology is unique, as she deviates from other theologians who portray Jesus as a Dalit or a servant. Singh comments that "rather than the image of a God who loves people because they are poor, Bama invokes an image of God who calls the poor to rise above their poverty and oppression."[37]

## Missing Themes

### Ecclesiology

Though Dalit theology has focused on new conceptions of God and Jesus Christ, they have ignored many other themes that had a lot of potential for Dalit liberation.

First, Dalit theologians have not challenged the ecclesiology that have perpetuated Dalit adversity through caste discrimination. Though the pioneers of Dalit theology had a vision of transforming church structures, it was never fulfilled. Nirmal says, "A vision of Dalit theology must also transform our ecclesiastical structures and must strive to usher in God's *shalom*."[38] The church remained the same, and the Dalit theologians who followed Nirmal ignored this aspect of the Dalit theological enterprise.

As Nelavala says, Dalit theology has not made any impact on the ecclesiastical scenario or the masses. As she puts it, "Since its emergence, a paradigm shift in theological studies in India has taken place under the influence of Dalit theology, but it has had negligible impact on ecclesiastical faith communities."[39]

Other Dalit feminist theologians also followed suit in criticizing ecclesiastical structures. Both Bama and Anderson have come out against

---

36  Surekha Nelavala, "Visibility of Her Sins. Reading the 'Sinful Woman' in Luke 7:36–50 from a Dalit Feminist Perspective," in Clarke, Deenabandhu, and Peacock, *Dalit Theology*, 262.

37  Roja Singh, "Bama's Critical-Constructive Narratives: Interweaving Resisting Visible Bodies and Emancipatory Audacious Voice as TEXTure for Dalit Women's Freedom," in Clarke, Deenabandhu, and Peacock, *Dalit Theology*, 227.

38  Nirmal, "Doing Theology," 144.

39  Nelavala, "Martin Luther's Concept of Sola Scriptura," 68.

church structures and beliefs that put women at a disadvantage. Bama is a Christian Dalit woman. Though she had taken a vow as a Catholic nun, she left the order after being disillusioned by institutionalized Christianity. Her experience as a former Catholic nun helped her form her views on Christianity and the church.[40] Roja Singh thinks that in her writings, Bama considers Christianity as both a liberator and an oppressor.[41] However, in Bama's writing, she highlights the negative sides of Christianity, particularly Catholicism. She thinks that many of the emphases of Christianity serve the purpose of enslaving people. Singh comments that Bama saw that "Christianity's teachings on humility, servitude, and acceptance seem[ed] to reconstruct a paradigm of slavery. She states that her religious indoctrination had numbed her to the ill-treatment she faced as a Dalit nun."[42] Bama also believes that the church restricts the freedom of emotional expression. A Dalit woman who is battered cannot yell or cry aloud, since the catechism considers these as negative actions.[43] In Bama's analysis, the church limits the freedom that Dalits originally had, especially around marriage and divorce. The social norms of the Pariah community permit divorce and remarriage for both men and women, but the church takes that freedom away.

Another significant challenge to reexamine ecclesiology also comes from Dalit-feminist theologians like Anderson, who tries to articulate a womanist ecclesiology. She critiques the silence and insensitivity of the church, which is the body of Christ, and she likens the church to the skin of the body: "The skin that has to protect the insides of the body has lost its sensitivity, sense of role, and responsibility. Perhaps turning the body inside out will be a way of rejuvenating life into the dead cells in the skin of the church."[44]

She also calls for a reexamination of the beliefs of the church: "The theologies of the church, the doctrines of the church, need to be urgently examined to see whether they are thoroughly masculinized. Hope for change and transformation depends on the way the body is allowed to

40  She wrote in Tamil, her mother tongue. However, her major contributions are now translated into English for the benefit of the wider world. Bama is the pen-name of Mary Fatima Rani. See Shakti Batra, *Bama: Karukku (a Critical Study)* (Delhi: Surjeet, 2019), 44.

41  Singh, "Bama's Critical-Constructive Narratives," 226.

42  Singh, 219.

43  Singh, 225.

44  Anderson, "Turning Bodies Inside Out," 212.

speak out, speak for, speak against, speak to, and speak from—from
a position of marginality back to the centre, from a position of being
silenced to learning a new language of love and justice to speak for and
of liberation of all."[45]

Thus ecclesiology is an area that a liberation theology for India has to
deal with—it is the major blind side of Dalit theology.

## Pneumatology

One topic that is certainly absent from Dalit theology is the Holy Spirit.
Nirmal did mention this theme but did not venture into it. His pneumatology is brief and sketchy, and he admits he has not developed it
fully.[46] Besides Nirmal, Mohan Larbeer, in the first decade of Dalit theology, pointed out the importance of the Holy Spirit as a liberator, though
he did not venture to develop a pneumatology. He suggests that "while
much work has been done on the life and ministry, death and resurrection of Christ in terms of human liberation, the dynamic potential of the
biblical understanding of the Spirit for liberation is yet to be explored.
But every aspect of the experience of the forsaken, as for example in the
life of the Dalit, is touched by the teaching on the Spirit."[47]

However, Dalit theology has not followed up on these proposals,
and other Dalit theologians seem to have ignored this topic altogether.
Dalit theology is silent about the person and work of the Holy Spirit.
How should a subjugated community understand the mission of the Holy
Spirit? What does the empowerment of the Holy Spirit mean to them?
These are still uncharted territory in Dalit theology. Pneumatology is significant for the Dalits, who have unique beliefs and experiences of the
supernatural. It is shocking to note that even critics have failed to point
out this lacuna in Dalit theology.

## Conclusion

The highly sophisticated hermeneutical methods of Dalit theologians
were beyond the reach of the Dalit masses. The sheer sophistication

---

45  Anderson, 213.

46  Nirmal, "Towards a Christian Dalit Theology," 69.

47  Mohan P. Larbeer, "The Spirit of Truth and Dalit Liberation," *Ecumenical Review*
42, no. 34 (1990): 233.

prevented Dalits from being the interpreters of their own knowledge and experience as envisaged by the founders. Besides the sophistication, Dalit hermeneutics limited itself mostly to the interpretation of the biblical text and its themes. This method evolved into reading the Bible from the perspective of the suffering of the Dalits. However, even while engaging in the hermeneutics of biblical texts, Dalit theologians do not question the text as feminist theologians do. The feminist hermeneutical approach is informed by the assumption that the Bible is the product of a patriarchal society; as the product of a patriarchal society, it is biased against women. Dalit theologians do not have such presuppositions about the text.

Though Dalit theologians are deeply occupied with biblical texts, they do not seem to have used the Bible adequately to challenge the caste system or other realities that oppress the Dalits. There is an immense textual resource in the Bible that theologians could have used to challenge the caste system, which is the structure of oppression. However, this was not done.

Dalit theologians who emulated the liberation theologians in the West did not realize that their contexts are radically different from each other. The liberation theologies of the West were justified in their reinterpretation of the Bible, since readings of the Bible created the pathos they were trying to address. As H. M. Conn observes, "The most basic source of liberation theology is the experience of poverty, destitution and repression in a region which Christendom has dominated for centuries." For him, liberation theology "constitutes a moral imperative for the Christian conscience." Conn cites liberation theologian Juan Luis Segundo of Uruguay: "Do not forget that we live at the same time in one of the most Christian lands and in one of the most inhumane ones."[48] Black theology addresses the white Christian interpretation of Christian faith that created and perpetuated Black pain. Similarly, liberation theology in Latin America is a conversation between traditional Christian interpretations that created the social reality that liberation theology was trying to dismantle.

However, the case of India is different. Christian and non-Christian Dalit scholars engaged in advocacy for the Dalits do not blame the Bible or its interpreters for the Dalits' predicament. They are unanimous that the pre-Christian concepts of Indian society, perpetuated by the Hindu

---

48  H. M. Conn, *New Dictionary of Theology* (Leicester: IVP, 1988), s.v. "Liberation Theology," 388.

scriptures and texts like *Manusmriti*, are responsible for caste discrimination and its attendant social injustice. Though this is the case, Dalit hermeneutics did not venture outside the Bible to the Hindu scriptures that created and perpetuate Dalit pathos. This observation led Clarke to propose that Dalit theology should engage in the deconstruction of the worldview of the dominant communities that produced Dalit pathos.[49]

Moreover, Dalit theologians also have a very narrow view of the discipline of hermeneutics. First, hermeneutics is not limited to written texts as popularly held, though in its origin, hermeneutics was viewed as a way to understand written texts. However, over the years, the discipline has expanded to include the interpretation of any social phenomenon—such as historical traditions, nature, science, law, and the like—that impinges on human existence.[50] As S. Lourdunathan points out, the relevance of hermeneutics grew to include the interpretation of any "meaningful social phenomenon, including complex (multi-texted) social phenomena like historical traditions or, one might add, (scientific) research traditions."[51]

Liberation happens when the oppressed question the hermeneutics that enslave them and find new meanings and possibilities for their existence. The task of theologians is to help the oppressed in this hermeneutical task by questioning, rereading, and deconstructing all the oppressive textual and nontextual systems that enslave them. Dalit theologians have mostly ignored the issue of Dalit worldviews that are oppressive and make them willing subjects of oppression, including the fear of evil powers that cause sickness, poverty, and so on. Hermeneutics should not end with the written texts—biblical or nonbiblical—but explore all that oppresses.

Hermeneutics is very natural to human beings. We are constantly engaged in finding meaning in our lives and the society we live in. Hermeneutics is a pathbreaking movement. As Lourdunathan puts it, "Humans characterized as physical, psychological, rational, emotional, aesthetic, devotional, is fundamentally hermeneutical."[52] Every human being is constantly defining themselves in their context.

---

49  Clarke, "Dalit Theology," 25.
50  For the latest range of subjects and disciplines that come under the ambit of hermeneutics, see Michael N. Forster and Kristin Gjesdal, *The Cambridge Companion to Hermeneutics* (Cambridge: Cambridge University Press, 2019).
51  S. Lourdunathan, *Hermeneutics of Dalit Philosophy of Liberation* (Tamil Nadu, India: Vergal, 2015), 5.
52  Lourdunathan, 5.

The narrow view of hermeneutics makes Dalit theologians ignore the structures behind the Dalit predicament. Dalit theology has failed to address the systems and agents of the Dalits' dilemma. For example, there is no theology against the oppressive caste system, which perpetuates discrimination. The Dalits also accept the caste system by subjecting themselves to it and promulgating it by discriminating against caste groups distinct from them, particularly the lower castes.

Dalit hermeneutics led to themes that need further elaboration. I have already noted the limitations of an exclusively incarnational theology. Also, over the years, there has been an emerging criticism of this approach among Dalit liberation theologians, since it had no potential for liberation. While fixated on an incarnational Christology, Dalit hermeneutics lost sight of other aspects of Christology that could have been the building blocks of a theology of liberation and integral transformation like ecclesiology and pneumatology.

Why did Dalit theology stall in its theological methods and themes and fail to venture into new horizons? Part of the answer seems to be in its isolation. It tried to sail alone, ignoring the trails made by the fleet ahead. Tagging along for some distance would have given it the momentum vital for its journey onward.

# 3

# A THEOLOGY
# IN ISOLATION

We're all islands shouting lies to each other across seas of
misunderstanding.

—Rudyard Kipling

Isolation is a self-defeating dream.

—Carlos Salinas de Gortari

We have already noted that Dalit theology is rooted in the tradition of
contextual and liberation theologies. Naturally, it draws a lot from the
liberation theologies of the time in terms of methodologies, themes, and
so on. Despite this continuity with other contextual and liberation theologies, Dalit theology is also a theology secluded in its immediate context.

## Discontinuity with Earlier "Dalit Theologies"

Though we credit A. P. Nirmal for the inauguration of Dalit theology
in the 1980s, it is wrong to assume that there were no theological reflections *by* the Dalits, *for* the Dalits, or *about* the Dalits before this point in
history. Before modern Dalit theology emerged in the 1980s, there were
many streams of Dalit theology, which for the lack of a better word I
would call "proto-Dalit theologies."

Though Dalit theology poised itself as counter to theologies of the
alleged Brahmanical traditions, Indian Christian theology was not limited
to Brahmanical traditions as might be presumed. There were at least two

other streams of theological reflection on Dalit issues in India: the first by European missionaries and the second by Christian converts from Dalit backgrounds. Dalit theology in its three modes—pathetic, empathetic, and sympathetic—was in existence in these streams. In their enthusiasm to counter the theologies of the alleged Brahmanical tradition, and to emulate the contextual liberation theologies thriving in the West, Dalit theologians ignored this wealth of Christian theological reflection on Dalits in their own neighborhood.

In the following pages, I would like to highlight the rich tradition that the Dalit theologians overlooked, taking a few representative samples; a detailed survey of these contributions must be the subject of further studies.

## Dalit Theology of the European Missionaries

Precursors of Dalit theology can be seen in the works of European missionaries before Indian independence. Several Western missionaries of the colonial period had been keen on theological reflection in light of their experience with the Dalits. There is an enormous cache of literature that the Western missionaries produced on the lives, rituals, and conditions of the Dalits in India. These are preserved in the books they authored and the correspondence between the missionaries and their sponsoring bodies in the sending countries. Sadly, most of these are lost to us or inaccessible, since they are still in the archives of various mission organizations abroad, waiting to be cataloged and made public. However, whatever is available has profound insights to offer.

## Bishop Daniel Wilson of Calcutta

One of the many notable contributions to theological reflections about Dalits came from Bishop Daniel Wilson of Calcutta (1778–1858). Wilson's theology is based on a sympathetic knowledge of the Dalit condition. As the bishop of a vast area stretching from Calcutta to present Sri Lanka, his engagement was mostly administrative rather than grassroots-level evangelism. He was a great man capable of theological reflection on social issues. His theological reflections were honed by his association with social reformers like William Wilberforce, the leading figure in the antislavery movement in Great Britain. He was also a member of the "Clapham sect," a reformist movement, along with reformers like

Charles Grant, Zachary Macaulay, and Wilberforce. In fact, he was pastor to Macaulay and Wilberforce at St. John's Bedford Row in England.

Wilson was forthright in opposing caste and its evils in society. He argued that the gospel of Jesus Christ envisages a society without caste. In his letter dated July 5, 1833, addressed to all the churches in India and Ceylon (present-day Sri Lanka), he says, "The gospel recognizes no distinctions such as those of castes, imposed by a heathen usage, bearing in some respect a supposed religious obligation."[1]

Wilson also found that caste in the church was against the fellowship of love and a hindrance to Christian mission. He stated that castes put "an immovable barrier against all general advance and improvement in society" and was responsible for cutting "asunder the bonds of human fellowship on the one hand and preventing those of Christian love on the other."[2]

Bishop Wilson considered caste consciousness not just a social or cultural issue but a theological one. Wilson equated the caste issue with the attempts of Judaizers in the early churches to distract converts from Christ to the old covenant and its religious ways. His letters to the Tamil Christians, where caste discrimination was at its peak, were couched in biblical metaphors and imagery. In one of his letters (March 27, 1834), he condemns those who perpetuated caste practices (despite the ban he imposed) in the church as those who have "separated themselves from the Lord that bought them, they have preferred Belial to Christ, they have resolved to mix the doctrine of the Holy Jesus with the dogmas of a heathenish superstition."[3]

Besides a theology of caste, Wilson also had an ecclesiology that challenged the caste practices of the churches. He writes, "Those who retain their caste are not properly and truly members of Christ's body at all. They 'halt between two opinions.'"[4] Wilson saw caste practice as a sign of defective spirituality. In one of his letters to the "native churches," he writes, "The question of Caste is a subordinate one in itself. It is as a symptom that it is important. It proves the diseased and feeble state of the spiritual life amongst you. I have given my judgment against it."[5]

---

1 Josiah Bateman, *The Life of the Right Rev. Daniel Wilson, D. D., Late Lord Bishop of Calcutta and Metropolitan of India* (London: J. Murray, 1861), 345.

2 Bateman, 345.

3 Bateman, 243.

4 Bateman, 243.

5 Bateman, 244.

Wilson called the caste practice an evil tie with paganism and alien to the gospel. He argued that conversion meant a separation from the world that perpetuated the evils of caste, since caste is "the evil of a voluntary tie kept up with the pagan world." He held that the practice of caste in the churches, as in society, was "the evil of a retreat to idolatry left open to the weak convert" and "the evil of a temptation to a lapse from Christianity to heathenism."[6]

Another important aspect of Wilson's theology is that he went beyond caste practices in the church and society to a theology that touches upon public life. According to Wilson, the meaningful future of Dalit Christians depends on their involvement in the Indian reality.[7] Clearly, Wilson advocated a theology that considers political involvement to improve the Dalits' condition.

## Henry Whitehead

In the same line of Bishop Wilson was the contribution of another Anglican—Bishop Henry Whitehead (1853–1947). This Anglican bishop of the Madras diocese was an important theologian in the colonial period who produced theological reflections on the Dalits. He was an academic of a great legacy, besides being a noted writer and churchman who published widely about India and the church in India.[8]

Whitehead's theology was concerned more with political and social realities than the spiritual aspects of human existence. Hebden points out that "perhaps Henry Whitehead's ideology of mission gives the earliest example of theology *for* Dalit Christians."[9] Whitehead reinterpreted the Puritan spiritual language to apply to the social reality in India. For example, as Hebden points out, he reinterpreted the "slough of despond" of John Bunyan's *The Pilgrim's Progress* (seventeenth century) to apply to the social mire rather than the spiritual bog the Christian pilgrim sinks into

6  Bateman, 244–45.
7  K. Wilson, "Towards a Humane Culture," in Nirmal, *Reader in Dalit Theology*, 168.
8  Whitehead was educated in Sherborne and Trinity College, Oxford. He was the principal of Bishops College, Calcutta, from 1883 to 1899. He became the fifth bishop of Madras in 1899 and served in that capacity for twenty-three years. His brother was the noted philosopher Alfred North Whitehead, and his son J. H. C. Whitehead became a famous mathematician.
9  Hebden, *Dalit Theology*, 72. See also Henry Whitehead, *Work among Indian Outcastes* (London: Society for Promoting Christian Knowledge, 1912).

under the weight of his sin. Whitehead was politicizing the gospel so that it would be relevant to the social reality he witnessed in India.

Whitehead was involved in hermeneutical tasks on behalf of the Dalits decades before modern Dalit theology emerged. Hebden also points out that Whitehead read the story of the exodus in the same way as liberation theologies long before Latin American liberation theologians ever attempted such a reading. For Whitehead, exodus is not salvation from sin, as popularly understood then, but a liberation from oppressive structures.[10]

While Bishops Wilson and Whitehead represent the mainline Anglican traditions, there were many voices from other church traditions that stood for the Dalit cause in the church and society.

### John S. Hoyland

Another important theological contribution in favor of the Dalits came from John S. Hoyland, who was a Quaker missionary to India from Great Britain. Most of his work was as an educator in different colleges in India. His involvement with Dalit students in the colleges where he taught or served as hostel warden led him to serious theological reflections about their condition. Most of his theological reflections are presented in the form of prayers, poems, and liturgies.

While Bishop Wilson's contribution has to do with the condition of Dalits in the churches—particularly the issue of segregation—Hoyland focused on producing theological resources by writing liturgy and prayer books to support the Dalit cause in society. He tried to awaken Dalit Christian minds (especially those of the Dalit students in his care) through written prayers.[11] Hebden comments that "J.S. Hoyland attempted to be in solidarity with the poor because he believed that God has a preferential option for the poor and oppressed."[12]

Hoyland can also be considered as a precursor to later Dalit Christology. He is the first to identify Jesus as a servant and a Dalit long before the later Dalit theologians developed their Christology around these images.

---

10  Hebden, *Dalit Theology*, 72.
11  John S. Hoyland, *A Book of Prayers: Written for Use in an Indian College* (London: Challenge Book and Picture Store, 1951), 49, cited in Hebden, *Dalit Theology*, 76.
12  Hebden, *Dalit Theology*, 77.

Hebden comments that "for Hoyland, 'Jesus is Dalit' although he lacks access to the term itself."[13]

Like many other European missionaries who confronted the Dalit predicament, Hoyland also had a theology that addressed public affairs. Very much in tune with the Quaker tradition, Hoyland used his faith to critique the British Empire in India. In his book published in 1943 (four years before India became independent in 1947), he argued that British rule in India was a failure. He advocated for mass education and abolition of communal voting and argued that a constitutional assembly should be set up and imperialism ended.[14]

Hoyland's theological reflections were rooted in his deep empathetic knowledge of suffering. He was directly involved in relief work during the influenza epidemic in India in 1918, for which he was awarded the Kaiser-i-Hind Gold Medal.[15] Hoyland also wrote a poem on the epidemic that he reported.[16]

### Bernard Lucas

Bernard Lucas (1860–1920) focused on the Dalits and their struggles. At a time when the Western missionaries were fixated on high-caste Hindus and their scriptures—studying their language and philosophy—Lucas advocated for the need to focus on the Dalits and their lives. He says, "The development of religious life of the Pariah and his salvation from degradation of centuries, are as important and as much a duty of the Christian Church, as any ministry to the religious life of the Brahmin and other caste people. In a sense this ministry is more important, for his need is greater and he has suffered greater neglect."[17]

In addition to Dalit issues, he addressed issues pertinent to Dalit conditions. Hebden points out that "Lucas introduces themes for Dalit theologians in the twentieth century to explore theological imperialism, dogmatism

13  Hebden, 77.
14  John S. Hoyland, *Indian Crisis; the Background* (Freeport, NY: Books for Libraries, 1970).
15  "Correspondence of John S. Hoyland (1887–1957), Quaker and Missionary, 1820–1958," Archives Hub, accessed November 19, 2019, https://archiveshub.jisc.ac.uk/data/gb159-ms733.
16  John S. Hoyland, *Letters from India* (London: Swarthmore Press, 1919), 82–83.
17  Bernard Lucas, *Our Task in India: Shall We Proselytise Hindus or Evangelise India?* (repr.; London: Macmillan, 1914), 44, cited in Hebden, *Dalit Theology*, 76.

over praxis and the foreignness of Christianity needing to shift from European colonialism to cosmic-foreignness."[18] He persuasively argued for human equality and dignity. Lucas wrote in 1909 that Christianity should not accept the limitations of race and nation but deal with man as man.[19]

Like some of his European counterparts, Lucas was also a theologian who addressed public issues. His book *The Empire of Christ* was a critique of the British Empire.[20] In this work, he explores issues like imperialism, dogmatism, and the foreignness of Christianity.

Besides a few samples that I have cited here, there are many who spoke to the Dalit condition even though the word *Dalit* was unknown to them. Some Western missionaries were involved in deconstructing the Hindu myths that promoted caste and Dalit oppression. Kondasingu Jesurathnam cites A. C. Hogg and Richard DeSmet as examples of Western Christian missionaries who tried to demystify the karmic theory that subjugated the Dalit mind.[21]

## Dalit Theology of the Natives

Just as converts from high-caste Hinduism were writing Indian Christian theology, Dalit Christians were also active theologians in the same period. They are less known until recently, and their voices had a limited impact on Christian academia, as they wrote in regional languages, unlike the foreign missionaries. Many of the contributions of Dalit Christians are lost to us, since they were oral in nature, and there is practically no documentation or preservation of their written works. Aleaz has documented

---

18  Hebden, *Dalit Theology*, 74.

19  Bernard Lucas, *Christ and Society* (London: Francis Griffiths, 1909), 11.

20  Bernard Lucas, *The Empire of Christ* (Charleston: BiblioBazaar, 2008).

21  See Jesurathnam, *Dalit Liberative Hermeneutics*, 164; A. G. Hogg, *Karma and Redemption: An Essay toward the Interpretation of Hinduism and the Re-statement of Christianity* (Madras, India: Christian Literature Society, 1970); William Richey Hogg, "Psalm 22 and Christian Mission: A Reflection," *International Review of Mission* 77, no. 306 (April 1988): 238–46; A. G. Hogg, *The Christian Message to the Hindu—Being the Duff Missionary Lectures for 1945 on the Challenge of the Gospel in India* (London: SCM, 2010); Richard DeSmet, "Fleeting Time and Sacrificially Produced Continuity in Vedic Brahmanism and in Early Christianity," *Indian Theological Studies* 19, no. 2 (1982): 119–44; and Richard DeSmet, "Job's 'Insufferable Comforters' and the Law of Karma," *Vidyajothi Journal of Theological Reflection* 5 (1994): 308–18.

some Dalit Christian movements led by Dalit Christians in South India during the colonial period.[22]

For example, Kumara Guru (also known as Poykayil Appachan) in Kerala is an example of one of the Dalit Christians who protested discrimination in society and church by establishing his own religious sect of Dalits known as the Prathyaksha Raksha Daiva Sabha. Born in 1879 to a Dalit family, he later converted to Christianity and joined the church as a preacher. However, he left the church in protest of its caste discrimination and established his own religious sect. He gave voice to his thoughts and protests in the form of songs and poems in Malayalam.[23]

One Dalit theological contributor whose work is rather well documented and discussed is G. Joshua (1895–1971), also known as Gurram Jashuva in Telugu. Joshua was born to Christian parents—his mother belonged to a cobbler (Dalit untouchable) caste, and his father was a Yadava (high caste). However, though he was entitled to be considered as high caste by virtue of his father being high caste, society considered him an untouchable Dalit. He is a typical example of Dalit Christian thinking before modern Dalit theology was born in the early 1980s. As a Dalit Christian poet in Telugu, he wrote thirty volumes of poetry during his half century of literary activity.[24] His poems touched on the social issues that the Dalits experienced. Prabhakar points out that though he was not trained in theology, Joshua's works were "quite in accordance with Christian Theology."[25]

He had a Christology that exalted Christ above the gods of his ancestors. For Joshua, Jesus Christ is great because he is the only God who accepts worship from the untouchables.[26] Joshua not only gave expression to his Christian faith but also critiqued high-caste Hindu society in light of his faith. His most famous work, *Gabbilam* (The Bat), is a critique of

---

22 Aleaz, "Expressions of Dalit Christian Identity."

23 P. Sanal Mohan, "Religion, Social Space and Identity: The Prathyaksha Raksha Daiva Sabha and the Making of Cultural Boundaries in Twentieth Century Kerala," *South Asia: Journal of South Asian Studies* 28, no. 1 (April 1, 2005): 35–63.

24 K. Gangaiah, "Emergence of Dalit Movements in Andhra and Dr. B. R. Ambedkar's Influence," *Proceedings of the Indian History Congress* 68, no. 1 (2007): 939.

25 M. E. Prabhakar, "Doing Theology with Poetic Traditions of India with Special Reference to the Dalit Poetry of Poet-Laureate, Joshua," in *Doing Theology with the Poetic Traditions of India: Focus on Dalit and Tribal Poems*, ed. Joseph Patmury (Bangalore: PTCA/SATHRI, 1996), 14.

26 Prabhakar, 12.

caste, untouchability, and inequality.[27] In his later works, Joshua gave voice to the Dalits who criticized the limitations of the church's structure and traditions that stood in the way of the Dalit cause.

"Proto-Dalit theology" was more than biblical interpretation. The work of early missionaries went beyond biblical hermeneutics and theologizing to social critique. Edgar Thompson, a Methodist missionary, saw that "the conscientization of the Dalits is the priority of rightly guided missionaries."[28]

The Dalit theology of the colonial period was the result of direct engagement with Dalit realities. A closer examination of the biographies or autobiographies of the European missionaries in India shows that the Dalit theology of the European missionaries evolved from their day-to-day engagement with the struggles of the Dalits. It was not merely academic reasoning untouched by ground realities.

One notable observation is that the European missionaries who wrote Dalit theology for and about the Dalits were of evangelical persuasion. Bishop Wilson was influenced by Wilberforce. John Hoyland was situated in the English Quaker tradition. Bernard Lucas was from the Christian Brethren background, and Thompson was Methodist. We should also note that the European missionaries addressed the issue of suffering but did not limit suffering to caste. Their concern was the suffering of humanity. However, the suffering they addressed happens to be that of the Dalits, who suffered due to their social location.

The survey leads us to conclude that modern Dalit theology cannot claim any monopoly over advocacy for Dalits. Dalit pathos was already the motivation for Dalit and non-Dalit religious thinkers to engage in intellectual discourse for the sake of the Dalits. However, the Dalit theology that emerged in the 1980s isolated itself from this great legacy of theological reasoning.

"Proto-Dalit theology" was not merely academic but led to action on the ground. Bishops Reginald Heber and Daniel Wilson were instrumental in banning caste practices in the churches under their jurisdiction. Proto-Dalit theology was also a public theology, as it addressed the evils of society. Proto-Dalit theology was deconstructionist. The colonial and even native theologians attempted to deconstruct karmic theory, social hegemony, and all that has caused Dalit pathos. The proto-Dalit theology

---

27  Prabhakar, 13.
28  Hebden, *Dalit Theology*, 73.

of the native Indian Christians also had a ring of critique of the evils of religion and of the Christian church.

## Isolation from Dalit Liberation Movements

Besides failing to draw inspiration from earlier theological reflections on the Dalits, Dalit theologians also ignored the Dalit movements that predated it, beginning in the sixth century BCE, from Buddha all the way to the present day. On the contrary, its siblings were very much rooted in the history of struggles and protests in their contexts. For example, Black theology was rooted in the US civil rights movement. Similarly, liberation theology in Latin America was also the offshoot of the base communities and the movements of the poor. Isabel Apawo Phiri points out that in South Africa, Black theology originated in the Black Consciousness movement.[29]

However, the Indian subcontinent also had Dalit movements, but Dalit theologians ignored them, depriving themselves of the sustenance and thrust they could have given. For example, the Dalit Panthers movement was already there when the Dalit theology movement began. The Dalit Panthers movement was founded on May 29, 1972, by Namdeo Dhasal and J. V. Pawar in Maharashtra, emulating the Black Panthers movement in North America. Though the movement began to lose its steam by the end of the 1980s, Dalit theology stood aloof from this movement. An association with the Dalit Panthers movement would have benefited both—it would have given Dalit Panthers a new lease on life and Dalit theology new winds in its sails.

Dalit theology seems to have nothing to do with Ambedkar's struggle for Dalits, which swayed the imagination of Dalits in the emerging independent India and continues its momentum even now in various Dalit assertion movements. Dalit theology also had no continuity with Ambedkar's movement or with his thoughts. John C. B. Webster points out that "Dalit Christian theologians have been making explicit use of Dr. Ambedkar," but Dalit Christian theology is "not derived directly from his thought."[30] Webster would ascribe any similarity between

---

29   Isabel Apawo Phiri, "Southern Africa," in Parratt, *Introduction to Third World Theologies*, 147.

30   John C. B. Webster, *Religion and Dalit Liberation: An Examination of Perspectives*, 2nd ed. (New Delhi: Manohar, 2002), 64.

Ambedkar's analysis and Dalit theology solely to Ambedkar's farsighted diagnosis and analysis of the Dalit Christian situation. Besides references to Ambedkar in works of Dalit theology, any active engagement with his thoughts about religion in general, Christianity, or liberation is lacking.

## Isolation from Dalit Discourse/Studies

Dalit theology starved itself through isolation from the wider academic discipline of Dalit studies and discourse. Dalit studies is a vibrant and growing academic discipline that explores the various aspects of Dalit existence, including Dalit history, culture, language, religion, and so on. This discipline understands the word *dalit* in a wider sense that includes all marginalized groups, such as the Dalits, tribals, minorities, women, and so on.

Dalit studies and Dalit discourse are so closely interrelated that scholars sometimes use these expressions interchangeably. The study of Dalit history and culture creates the discourse that is aimed at asserting Dalit identity and power. In other words, we can construe Dalit discourse as Dalit studies aimed at advancing the Dalit cause in all possible ways. However, the boundaries between the two disciplines are not blurred entirely; they are two interdependent disciplines. Notwithstanding all the common factors and distinctions, for the sake of convenience, I prefer to use the expression "Dalit discourse" in general unless I mean Dalit studies as a distinct, pure discipline.

According to Ramnarayan S. Rawat, "A key aim of Dalit studies is to recover histories of struggles for human dignity and caste discrimination by highlighting Dalit intellectual and political activism."[31] However, the discipline is much wider than recovering the histories of Dalit struggles. Dalit studies focuses on Dalit culture, politics, economics, spirituality, and so on.

Quite a wealth of literature exists in India on all these aspects. Though all these can still be split into specific disciplines, *Dalit studies* can be used as an umbrella term that encompasses all. Imtiaz Ahmad and

---

31 Ramnarayan Rawat, "The Rise of Dalit Studies and Its Impact on the Study of India: An Interview with Historian Ramnarayan Rawat," Historians, accessed January 27, 2020, https://www.historians.org/publications-and-directories/perspectives-on-history/summer-2016/the-rise-of-dalit-studies-and-its-impact-on-the-study-of-india-an-interview-with-historian-ramnarayan-rawat.

Shashi Bhushan Upadhyay have documented a wide spectrum of Dalit studies in their edited work.[32] Dalit studies includes Dalit art, literature, linguistics, and so on.[33] An example of Dalit studies in a wider sense is showcased in the writings of Kancha Ilaiah, a Dalit academic. He sheds light on many unique aspects of Dalit life, culture, economics, medicine, feminism, and so on.[34]

Dalit studies also explores the contributions of Dalits to Indian society that have been overlooked. Various works by Badri Narayan have explored the contributions of Dalits, particularly Dalit women, to Indian history and culture.[35]

Dalit theology and Dalit studies have many things in common. First, both have to do with the Dalit reality of suffering. While Dalit studies explores the natural and historical causes of Dalit realities to order a future course for Dalit advancement, Dalit theology sees the Christian God in Dalits' history and predicament. Theology is born at the intersection of the realities of human existence and faith in God. Dalit theology is what God has done and can do in the lives of the Dalits, but not all of Dalit studies may have this divine angle. Dalit theology can still be imagined as a subset of Dalit studies.

Being a possible subset of Dalit studies, Dalit theology should have been in conversation with Dalit studies to enrich itself. Since it has to do with the life of the Dalits, it must draw its inspiration and substance from the wider Dalit academic enterprise. Having surveyed the wealth of studies of Dalits, Sebastian proposes that Dalit theology must be multidisciplinary in nature. He suggests that "the strength of Dalit theology

---

32  Imtiaz Ahmad and Shashi Bhushan Upadhyay, *Dalit Assertion in Society, Literature and History* (New Delhi: Orient Blackswan, 2010).

33  Gary Michael Tartakov, *Dalit Art and Visual Imagery* (New Delhi: Oxford University Press, 2012); on linguistics, see Kaviyoor Murali, *Dalit Bhasha Nigandu (Dalit Language Lexicon)—Malayalam* (Kottayam, India: DC Books, 2010).

34  See, particularly, Ilaiah, *Post-Hindu India*.

35  See, particularly, Narayan, *Women Heroes*; Badri Narayan, *Fascinating Hindutva: Saffron Politics and Dalit Mobilisation* (New Delhi: Sage, 2009); Badri Narayan, "Imagining the Past and Reconstructing Histories," *Social Scientist* 35, nos. 9/10 (2007): 67–87; Badri Narayan, "History Produces Politics: The 'Nara-Maveshi' Movement in Uttar Pradesh," *Economic and Political Weekly* 45, no. 40 (2010): 111–19; Badri Narayan, *Documenting Dissent: Contesting Fables, Contested Memories and Dalit Political Discourse* (Shimla: Indian Institute of Advanced Studies, 2001); Badri Narayan, *Multiple Marginalities: An Anthology of Identified Dalit Writings* (New Delhi: Manohar, 2004); and Narayan, *Women Heroes*.

lies precisely in the possibility of its inter-disciplinarity, something that needs to be acknowledged and fostered."[36]

The pioneers of Dalit theology had envisaged a relationship between Dalit studies and Dalit theology, though they did not have access to the term *Dalit studies*. For example, Massey holds that Dalit history is an essential ingredient in Dalit theology. He proposes that "one of the dire needs while we are thinking about 'dalit theology' is 'dalit history.'"[37] Massey argues that three main requirements for a living theology are "life context, history and language."[38] Massey also suggests that Dalit theology must be written in the respective languages of the Dalits concerned.[39] When proposing Dalit theology as an academic discipline, Nirmal had also identified that one of the major problems in doing Dalit theology was a lack of knowledge of Dalit history. It was a clarion call that Dalit theology must be founded on the facts of history and experience of the Dalits. It should not be just imagined. Prabhakar wrote in 1988, "Dalit theology is *new theology* because it is from below and uses dalit peoples' language and expressions, their stories and songs of suffering and triumphs popular wisdom including their values, proverbs, folklore myths and so on to interpret their history and culture, and to articulate a faith to live by and to act on."[40] However, Dalit theology, as we have already seen, operated as a Christian discipline secluded from other disciplines concerning Dalits. Though founding father Nirmal tried to establish a dialogue with Dalit literature by establishing the Dalit Sahitya Academy, Dalit theologians in general stood aloof from the Dalit literature movement.[41]

Historically, Dalit theologians overlooked the organic link with Dalit studies and ignored the advice of the pioneers. It is a fact of history that Dalit theology unplugged itself from the wider discipline of Dalit studies. In 2010 (in the third decade of Dalit theology), noting this flaw in Dalit theology, Clarke remarked that Dalit theology must move forward from literal interpretations of the Bible to Dalit oral culture. He proposed that "instead of literal interpretations of biblical texts to address the complex

---

36  Sebastian, "Can We Now Bypass That Truth?," 84.
37  James Massey, "Ingredients for a Dalit Theology," in Nirmal, *Reader in Dalit Theology*, 148.
38  Massey, 147.
39  Massey, 148.
40  Prabhakar, "Search for a Dalit Theology," 47.
41  Nirmal, "Dialogue with Dalit Literature." Also Webster, *Religion and Dalit Liberation*, 67.

reality of Dalit pathos, more metaphorical and less literary hermeneutic conventions prevalent among such oral communities would need to be utilized for Dalit articulations on God."[42]

## Conclusion

Dalit theology was not supposed to be a voice in the wilderness as imagined. There was a wealth of theological reflection on the Dalits and the structures that oppressed them by both foreign and native theologians. These pioneers dared to challenge oppressive structures of caste and power besides challenging the status quo of the church. There were favorable winds when modern Dalit theology was born in the 1980s that would have propelled it and sustained its thrust. These theologians predating modern Dalit theology had laid the foundations for deconstructing the oppressive systems on which Dalit theology could have built a theological edifice. The non-Christian Dalit movements and Dalit studies could fuel and enrich theological reflection, taking Dalit theology to new horizons.

---

42  Clarke, "Dalit Theology," 31.

# 4

# THE DALIT REALITY

> They [Dalits] had become people stressing their own particularity,
> just as better-off groups in India stressed their particularities.
> —V. S. Naipaul

Assessing the efficacy of Dalit liberation theology also requires scrutiny of its perception of the Dalit reality. In the pages that follow, I explore the multifaceted Dalit reality that should guide our theological reflections. Did Dalit theology have a comprehensive view of the Dalit reality?

Words are important because they not only describe reality but also shape reality to a large extent. Human beings tend to believe that they are what others designate them to be. Down through the ages, different words described the sociopolitical entity that we now signify as the "Dalit." Each of these words carries its own connotations and betrays the users' own perceptions of the Dalit reality. Since the word *Dalit* is attested widely in Indian languages, its origin is supposed to be Sanskrit, the ancient Indian language.

Dalit liberation theology focuses on the pathos of the Dalits because it understands the word *Dalit* in its negative sense as "broken," "oppressed," and so on. Massey's word study of *Dalit* reinforced this sense to dominate Dalit hermeneutics ever since. Massey points out that the word *Dalit* in Hebrew means "broken." It is indisputably so. He cites Hebraists to say that the Hebrew word might have originated in the cognate languages of ancient West Asia. He further hypothesizes that Sanskrit and Hebrew have common ancestors in these ancient Semitic languages. From this, he establishes that the Sanskrit word must have the same meaning as the

Hebrew word in the sense of "broken."[1] Massey's suggestion has been so persuasive that most Dalit theologians working on biblical texts subscribe to his assumptions unquestionably.

However, the common ancestry of Hebrew and Sanskrit is not established and is doubtful. Moreover, Sanskrit scholars would find it impossible to narrow the meaning of the Sanskrit word *Dalit* to its meaning in Hebrew. On the contrary, Sanskrit lexicographers point out that the word could signify two rather contradictory realities. In Sanskrit, it could mean "open," referring to the blooming of flowers. At the same time, it could also mean "broken" or "crushed."[2]

There is almost a consensus that it is Mahatma Phule who used the word *Dalit* in Marathi to designate the underprivileged section of Indian society.[3] Most scholars also agree that Ambedkar popularized this word through his writings to undermine the rather patronizing word *Harijan*, which Mahatma Gandhi used.

It is possible that Phule, born into a family of royal gardeners, drew the word from his experience of plants and flowers. So it is highly probable that Phule used it in the sense of assertion as he envisioned the power of the lower castes to bloom and flourish. In his writings, he highlighted the power of the Dalits to overcome their adverse conditions, their power to emerge and to bloom. He proved his conviction in his own life by educating his own wife against the norms of society that denied education to children.

In Dalit discourse, the word *Dalit* is a self-designation to reject contemptuous and condescending designations. Indian writers, thinkers, and political and social pundits used an array of words to designate those who are on the lower rung of the caste system in India. Common among these terms are *Shudra*, *Dasa* or *Chandala*, *Untouchables*, *Harijans*, and *Scheduled Castes and Tribes*. Dalit leaders like Phule and his followers detested these words, leading them to coin a new word, *Dalit*, to portray them. Dalit thinkers also rejected these words as either contemptuous or condescending.

---

1 Massey, *Towards Dalit Hermeneutics*, 3.
2 Monier Williams, *A Sanskrit-English Dictionary: Etymologically and Philologically Arranged with Special Reference to Cognate Indo-European Languages* (New Delhi: Motilal Banarsidass, 1899).
3 Mahatma Phule was born on April 11, 1827, and died on November 28, 1890. Baba Saheb Ambedkar (April 14, 1891–December 6, 1956) was born a year after Phule died.

Though Dalit liberation theologians generally tend to use *Dalit* exclusively in the sense of brokenness, there are voices that appeal to its bivalence. For example, Clarke thinks that the word *Dalit* should not be used exclusively in the sense of their pitiable, broken estate. Clark finds three reasons for using the word *Dalit*. First, it is a word that expresses self-representation. Second, it expresses their condition of being oppressed, broken, or "crushed" and describes their lives. Moreover, the word "incorporates elements of a positive expression of pride and a resistive surge for combating oppression."[4]

Besides the diversity of its meaning, in contemporary political parlance, the word *Dalit* is much broader than its caste nuances. Badri Narayan notes that Dalit politicians have widened the scope of this word. As Narayan says, "In the context of contemporary Dalit politics, the term 'dalit' is a generic term including not only the untouchable (*achhut*) castes in the Hindu caste hierarchy, but also the socially undeveloped, oppressed, exploited lower castes that are not all untouchable. Thus, Dalits include SCs [Scheduled Castes], STs [Scheduled Tribes], the so-called criminal tribes, nomadic tribes, OBCs [Other Backward Classes] and other backward social groups."[5]

In the same vein, Ram Sharan also defines *Dalit* not as a caste but as a socioeconomic condition. He suggests that instead of considering it as the name of a traditional caste, it should designate "a social group which has been deprived of the rights which other sections of society enjoyed."[6] Anand Teltumbde, a leading Dalit thinker, points out that in contemporary parlance, *Dalit* has become a generic term that includes various low castes and subcastes.[7] *Dalit* is thus a word that represents all those who are victims of a variety of adversities imposed upon them.

Besides making *Dalit* more inclusive, political thinkers have also deployed synonyms like *Bahujan* to subvert the superiority of their oppressors. As the word *Bahujan* entered Indian political parlance, it almost replaced the word *Dalit*, at least for a while. Kanshi Ram, the Dalit leader

4  Sathianathan Clarke, "Hindutva, Religious and Ethnocultural Minorities, and Indian-Christian Theology," *Harvard Theological Review; Cambridge* 95, no. 2 (April 2002): 198–99.

5  Narayan, *Women Heroes*, 33.

6  Ram Sharan, "Dalits in India: In Historical Perspective of Caste System," *International Journal of Advanced Research in Management and Social Sciences* 1, no. 5 (2012): 5.

7  Anand Teltumbde, *Dalits: Past, Present and Future* (London: Routledge, 2016).

and politician who introduced this word, gave it a new twist to his political advantage and the upliftment of the Dalits. According to him, the word *Bahujan* comprises about six thousand castes in India, which represents 85 percent of the population. The Bahujan Samaj Party, which he launched in 1984, included SCs, STs, OBCs, and other backward communities, represented by this large segment of Indian population.[8] This made the disadvantaged people a majority and the Brahmanical groups a minority. But *Dalit* was so deeply etched in Indian consciousness that *Bahujan* could not replace it completely. The word *Dalit* in the widened sense subsumed the word *Bahujan*, though the name of the party that Ram founded still preserves it.

In summary, we may conclude that the word *Dalit* refers to both oppression and assertion—in other words, pain and power. As Christopher points out, it signifies "that which is emerging or unfolding (suggesting critical consciousness). Thus, it encompasses the twin meanings of oppression and assertion."[9] These two possibilities of the meaning of the word *Dalit* help us view the Dalit reality as one of pathos and power, which I explore further. Moreover, the word *Dalit* also signifies not only caste-based oppression but all those who are at various disadvantages in their own contexts.

## Dalit Pathos

Undeniably, Dalits are objects of violence. Violence against the lower castes is as old as caste-based thinking and behavior. According to reports, crimes against Dalits increased by 25 percent in the decade ending in 2016. The National Crime Records Bureau has recorded 25,455 crimes committed against Dalits in 2000. This means that every hour, two Dalits are assaulted; every day, three Dalit women are raped, two Dalits murdered, and two Dalit homes torched.[10] The violence against them is on the rise. According to statistics published by the same agency in 2020,

8  P. Muthaiah, "Politics of Dalit Identity," *Indian Journal of Political Science* 65, no. 3 (2004): 399.

9  Christopher, "Between Two Worlds," 23n1.

10  Rup K. Barman, "Caste Violence in India: Reflections on Violence against the Dalits of Contemporary India," *Voice of Dalit* 3, no. 2 (2010): 201.

there were nearly 46,000 crimes against them in 2019, which is up more than 7 percent in the previous year.[11] Violence against Dalits comes in various forms. According to Rup K. Barman, Dalits are the victims of social, cultural, civil, economic, communal/religious violence, violence against Dalit women, psychological and physical torture, and so on. Sociocultural violence manifests as social segregation, forcing people to do menial jobs, prohibition of marriage, and so on.[12]

### Agents of Dalit Violence

The blame for violence against Dalits generally falls on the Brahmanical power structures. The Brahmanical interpretation of some Hindu scriptures created a worldview that has dehumanized the Dalits. This has led to a situation in which they are treated as objects that can be violated.

The religious structures other than the Brahmanical power structures are also equally guilty of Dalit violence. The irony is that many times, they have become victims of violence by the very communities that they have converted to in order to escape casteism. According to statistics that Barman cites, there are around sixty million non-Hindu Dalits in India.[13] They are converts to Islam, Sikhism, and Christianity. Non-Hindu Dalits also face communal violence of different sorts from the religions that they have embraced.

The Christian church that practices caste is also a collaborator in violence against the Dalits. The Dalits who have converted to Christianity still carry the stigma of being Dalits. They are ill-treated in congregations and denominations where the Christians who claim high-caste status or origin control the hierarchy. The Christian Dalits suffer more, since they are also denied the reservation rights that other non-Hindu Dalits enjoy (free education, reservations in jobs, etc.). While Dalits in general and Dalit converts to other religions enjoy these special constitutional rights, Dalits who embrace Christianity lose all these the moment they make that move.

---

11  Statistics keep changing. The Crime Records Bureau of India updates the figures on its website, http://www.ncrb.gov.in, regularly.

12  Barman, "Caste Violence in India," 201–2.

13  For the distribution of the Dalit population in various religions of India, see Barman, 205.

The Christian church's apathy toward the Dalits is the main reason for Dalits being denied their constitutional rights. Scholars like P. Muthaiah point out that Christian members of the Constitutional Assembly were converts to Christianity from high castes who had no concern for Dalit converts to Christianity; they kept their peace when issues of Dalit converts were debated.[14]

There is every reason to think that the apathy of the church leadership toward the Dalits in the churches continues. According to Shiri, "Dalit converts to Christian faith are in a way caught up in a triangle of oppression":[15] first, by the society, which still considers them Dalits even after their change of religion; second, by the churches they have joined, which still consider them Dalits; and third, by the state, which denies them the privileges accorded to Dalit converts to other religions.

## Assimilation by the Dominant Groups

Another facet of Dalit pathos is the threat of assimilation by the dominant groups that have subjugated them historically. The assimilation of other non-Hindu groups to Hinduism is based on politician Vinayak Damodar Savarkar's understanding of Hindutva. Savarkar accepted all religious groups in India other than Christians and Muslims as Hindus.[16] In 1928, the political party Hindu Mahasabha passed a resolution to the effect that the untouchables have equal rights with other Hindus to education and share public facilities like roads and wells.[17] These ideological foundations inspired many attempts to incorporate tribals, Adivasis, and animists into the Hindu fold. The most notable of these movements is the Ghar Wapsi (homecoming) movement, which engages in conversion movements all over India among the tribals.

Indian history testifies that the depressed classes also made attempts to return to the Hindu fold through the census to claim greater dignity by enrolling themselves as Hindus. However, Dalit reformers like Ambedkar considered assimilation and return to the Hindu fold as a threat. In the Round Table Conference of 1931, Ambedkar demanded that the

---

14  Muthaiah, "Politics of Dalit Identity," 393.

15  Godwin Shiri, *Dalit Christians: A Saga of Faith and Pathos* (New Delhi: ISPCK/NCCI, 2012), 117.

16  Vinayak Damodar Savarkar, *Hindutva: Who Is a Hindu?* (Bombay, India: Veer Savarkar Prakashan, 1969).

17  Muthaiah, "Politics of Dalit Identity," 389–90.

untouchables be designated as Protestant Hindus or nonconformist Hindus.[18] His interest was in keeping a separate identity for the depressed classes independent of the Hindus.

Assimilation never brought dignity to the Dalits, but it was instead a new form of enslavement that perpetuated discrimination. Assimilation in any form is not to be confused with egalitarianism within the Hindu fold. It is an invitation to the stratification that has denied them their rights for ages. Since the Dalits and Adivasis who join (not return to) the Hindu religion are assigned castes, this in turn perpetuates caste discrimination and all its attendant evils. As Hebden rightly points out, the assimilation is "not a call to return to a true and ancient religion of India, but to a modern version of the Brahmanic faith that assimilates or marginalizes castes and communities for political ends."[19] In the process of assimilation, the Dalits lose their religious identity and culture as Dalit gods are replaced by the Vedic, Brahmanic gods. Lancy Lobo has documented cases of how Hindutva enslaves Dalits and tribals by influencing their culture.[20]

Dalit pathos is a reality, but it is multifaceted—social, economic, physical, cultural, and so on. To deny Dalit pathos is to ignore an important aspect of this reality. However, Dalit reality doesn't end with suffering.

## Dalit Power

Just as the meaning of the word *Dalit* is not limited to brokenness or pain, Dalit reality is not just limited to the suffering of the Dalits. History evidences that Dalits are a people of power as well. This means that any theology of liberation should take into account the inherent power of Dalits to liberate themselves. They should be incorporated into movements of liberation as collaborators and participants, not just objects or beneficiaries. While tracking the impact of Dalit liberation theology, Dheenabandhu Manchala proposes that Dalit pathos is limited in its

18  Muthaiah, 390.
19  Hebden, *Dalit Theology*, 45.
20  Lancy Lobo, *Religious Conversion and Social Mobility: A Case Study of the Vankars in Central Gujarat* (Surat, India: Centre for Social Studies, 1991). Hebden documents some of his experiences in this regard. Hebden, *Dalit Theology*, 46.

scope for theological reflection.[21] Their struggles for liberation and justice must also be the subject of theological reflection.

It is an undeniable fact of history that Dalits have contributed significantly to Indian culture and history. As Dalit writer Kancha Ilaiah says, "The socio-economic conditions and cultural processes of the tribals shows that they taught the 'essence of life' to the rest of the society." They are our teachers. Ilaiah goes on to say that "they [Dalits] laid the foundation of our culture and our civilization. They taught us what to eat and what to drink in order to survive."[22]

### Evidence of Dalit Power

Indian history testifies that the Dalits were not always downtrodden and deprived. Some celebrated rulers of India were of low caste origins. The Nanda dynasty (345–321 BCE) that ruled most of what we know as Bihar and Chhattisgarh was of Shudra origin. The Nanda dynasty was replaced by the Maurya dynasty. Chandragupta Maurya, the founder of the Maurya dynasty, was also of low caste origin. Since he married a Shudra woman called Durdhara, the kings of this dynasty, Bindusara, and Ashoka, were of Shudra origin as well. According to Nitish Sengupta, a confederation of low-caste rulers ruled over North Bengal. A ruler called Divya overthrew Mahipala II in the eleventh century. He was from the low caste called Jaliya Kaibarta. The successors of this ruler—namely, Rudak and Bhim—were also from the same caste. Their rule lasted for about fifty years.[23] Two brothers from the shepherd community (*Kuruba*)— Harihara and Bukkaraya—established the famous Vijayanagar Empire in 1336 CE.

Moreover, the crisis of warfare with the Muslim rulers created a situation whereby anyone who was able and willing to fight the enemy could elevate himself to a position of power irrespective of caste. Historians have established that by 1700 AD, 70 percent of the Hindu maharajahs were of Shudra origin. These include Shivaji, Surajmal, Ranjit Singh, Scindia,

---

21  Dheenabandhu Manchala, "Expanding the Ambit: Dalit Theological Contribution to Ecumenical Social Thought," in Clarke, Deenabandhu, and Peacock, *Dalit Theology*, 41.

22  Ilaiah, *Post-Hindu India*, 5.

23  Nitish K. Sengupta, *Land of Two Rivers: A History of Bengal from the Mahabharata to Mujib* (New Delhi: Penguin, 2011).

Holkar, and others.[24] Though these political and military achievers are of low caste origin, the social system that assigned caste by achievement might have considered them as Khashtriyas, or warriors.

Historically, Dalits have proven their spirit for freedom and dignity. Among many stories of the fight for dignity and freedom is the story of Sammakka, Sarakka (her daughter), and Jampanna (her son), which is largely forgotten. They resisted the expansion of the Kakatiya dynasty into their territory in the thirteenth century CE.[25] Similarly, Komaram Bheem also resisted the Nizam of Hyderabad. He organized movements against the Nizam's policies of forest and revenue in the 1920s and '30s.[26] These Dalit movements are dated before those of Shivaji, Bal Gangadhar Tilak, and M. K. Gandhi, who educated Indians to fight against the expansionist forces in their territories—external enemies like the Mughals and the European colonial powers.

Dalits were not only safeguarding their own interests; they were active participants in India's struggles for freedom. A significant number of Dalit heroes participated in freedom struggles. Badri Narayan has documented the shrines and memorials erected all over Uttar Pradesh to commemorate the Dalit heroes who took part in the revolt of 1857.[27] Narayan reports that Dalit women also played a significant role in the fight for independence in 1857.

Though the leadership of Jawaharlal Nehru and M. K. Gandhi and others is highlighted, the history of the struggle for independence is dotted with Dalit leaders at local levels. Some of the Dalits who were involved in these struggles are Sengya Sambudhan, Rani Gaidinliu, Birsa Munda, Laxman Nayak, Sanjibhai Rupjibhai Delkar (freedom fighter and first Member of Parliament of Dadra and Nagar Haveli), Komaram Bheem, Sidhu Murmu, Kanhu Murmu, and others. Besides these, we also must recognize many unnamed tribals and Dalits who fought along with Pazhassi Raja, Shivaji, and others.

---

24  Among the many works on the history of ancient India, for works that focus on Dalit contributions to ancient Indian politics, see Burjor Avari, *India: The Ancient Past: A History of the Indian Subcontinent from c. 7000 BCE to CE 1200* (London: Routledge, 2016); and Sanjeev Sanyal, *Land of the Seven Rivers: A Brief History of India's Geography* (New Delhi: Penguin, 2012).

25  Ilaiah, *Post-Hindu India*, 18.

26  Ilaiah, 19.

27  Narayan, *Women Heroes*.

## Historical Background of Dalit Power

Dalit power has a long historical background. The battles with the Dasya documented in the Vedas show that the Dalits were combating the forces against them. However, we do not know the details of these battles in which the people of the land fought against invaders.

As early as the second half of the first millennium, Buddhism and other heterodox sects were upholding the cause of those on the lower rungs of society. They were also advancing the cause of those oppressed by stifling social systems that operated against their social advancement. These sects, including Jainism, dating to the sixth century BCE were movements against social stratification and its attendant social problems; they opposed Brahmanism by enabling Dalit liberation and assertion.

Historian of ancient India Romila Thapar argues that according to Buddhist teachings, society has fallen from a pristine utopian state to reach its present nadir of pain and suffering, but it also hopes that society will rise again back to its initial utopian state.[28] Thapar opines that "in the case of the Buddha, the emphasis on 'the middle way,' the path devoid of excesses, emphasizing moderation and a moral life, was indicative of his concern that the path suggested by him be compatible with the real problems of social existence."[29] She further points out that Buddha did accept casteism, but only as the framework of a socioeconomic structure; he rejected its attendant evil notions of purity and pollution, which discriminated against people.[30]

Buddha had a hermeneutic of deconstruction of the Hindu doctrines. As part of his social protest, Buddha rejected the ills of the doctrine of karma, arguing that though karma is the reason for our present condition, no person is bound to their karma forever. Teaching that the individual is ultimately responsible for their condition in their present life and future lives, the theory of karma eliminated the concept of social justice and social protests. Karmic theory also taught that rejecting or protesting one's fate is "bad karma" that will have consequences in this life and future lives.[31] The people who suffered could not even blame gods for their fate, since their condition was of their own making. But Buddha

28  Romila Thapar, "Ethics, Religion, and Social Protest in the First Millennium B.C. in Northern India," *Daedalus* 104, no. 2 (1975): 125.

29  Thapar, 124–25.

30  Thapar, 126.

31  Thapar, 126.

emphasized that the power to overcome karma rests with the individual. Buddha taught that the destiny of any person can be changed by observing the precepts of dharma or the Eightfold Path (or the law) as taught by Buddha.[32]

The doctrine of dharma that Buddha promoted was also a form of social protest. The Buddhist idea of dharma, in place of gods, is another method of social protest to bring equality. This helped people free themselves of caste-specific cults and promoted a universal religion transcending caste.

Buddha's doctrine of ahimsa, or nonviolence, also had social implications that favored the Dalit cause. Thapar contends that ahimsa is not an aspect of pacifism, but it is a social protest.[33] It is a conciliatory ethic against social evils. By opposing the sacrifice of animals, it tried to stifle Vedic Brahmanism, which thrived on animal sacrifice, as they were the sole ritual experts. The doctrine of ahimsa was a way of promoting an anti-Brahmanical lifestyle and their vocation. It also aimed to stop inter-tribal warfare. Consequently, nonviolence offered equal opportunities for all, as it helped the expansion of settled agriculture and trade activities, which benefited everyone in the society.[34] Buddha's doctrine of ahimsa also had sociopolitical dimensions, as it checked the process of political authoritarianism, which turned Janapadas into kingdoms by conquests.[35] It tried to check the growth of authoritarian kingdoms where social injustice and inequalities reigned.

Buddhism took practical steps to erase caste identities from society. In the Buddhist monasteries, caste identities were erased and replaced with new names without caste references. Thapar also points out that the adoption of vegetarianism in Buddhist orders was also a way of removing caste segregation based on food habits and rules.[36]

By turning Buddhist monasteries into learning centers, Buddha dismantled the Brahmanical monopoly on learning and being the sole custodians of knowledge. Education was thus open to all who desired it. Buddhism released the creativity of those who were once suppressed, which thus made a lasting impact on Indian philosophy, culture,

---

32  Thapar, 125.
33  Thapar, 128.
34  Thapar, 127.
35  Thapar, 127.
36  Thapar, 128.

language, art, and so on. The choice of language itself shows the anti-Brahmanical stance of Buddhism. To make his appeal popular, he chose *ardha-maGadhi*—a prakrit of the Middle Ganges Plain. Thapar notes that at a time when the Brahmanical culture was seeking an *Aryan* identity and exclusivity, Buddha was deliberately shunning it.[37]

Buddhism in its teachings and practices is a movement that asserted the rights of the victims of caste-based oppression and their equality with the rest of society. We don't have any statistics to prove how many people who belonged to lower castes joined these movements to protest inequalities and claim equality in society. However, the appeal of Buddhism over the centuries, even testified by the neo-Buddhist movement that Ambedkar founded, means that it was a powerful witness to Dalit assertion over the social and religious systems that subjugated them.

### Expressions of Dalit Power

Among the many manifestations of Dalit power are the Bhakti movements that have protested social inequalities since the eighth century. Most of the Bhakti poets and sages were from Dalit backgrounds and were severe social critics too. Through their songs, a whole array of saints advocated for the right of the "untouchables" to worship in the temple. These include Chokamela, Namdev, Tuka Ram, Kabir Das, and so on. As Paramjit S. Judge remarks, "In the form of the Bhakti movement, the plausibility of questioning the power of the upper castes within the framework of Hindu ideology of dharma/karma was realised."[38]

A good example is Kabir Das (1440–1518), a Dalit who composed poems in Hindi to address the evils in his society, particularly the evil of untouchability. His social critique makes Kabir stand out among the saints of his time. While some of his famous contemporaries—Surdas, Tulsidas, and Mirbai—composed songs of devotion to their chosen gods, Kabir turned toward humanity and its suffering. He questioned those who were responsible for the suffering. He confronted the teachers, religious leaders, and laity with probing questions.

The tradition of Kabir continues in contemporary India as a means of Dalit assertion, particularly through the mission singers in Punjab.

---

37  Thapar, 130.
38  Paramjit S. Judge, "Between Exclusion and Exclusivity: Dalits in Contemporary India," *Polish Sociological Review* 2, no. 178 (2012): 266.

Santosh K. Singh reports that since 2009, Punjab has seen a new cultural movement where Dalit singers assert themselves against the upper-caste Jatt Sikhs through their songs in audio and video formats. They are called mission singers because their aim is not to make money but to propagate the teachings of Dalit saints and heroes, including Ambedkar.[39] Such movements are reported in other parts of the country as well.

The reform movements of various Dalit leaders are further evidence of Dalit power. The reform movements of Dalit leaders are a pan-Indian phenomenon. The main social reformers among them are Jyotirao Phule (1827–90) in western India, Narayana Guru (1855–1928) in Kerala, Vagya Varma Reddy in Andhra Pradesh, Panchanan Barma (1865–1935), and Thakur Harichand (1811–77) and his son Guru Chand Thakur in Bengal. Each of these reform movements also were movements of Dalit assertion to a large extent that raised many Dalit leaders to fight their cause. The contributions of these Dalit social reformers resulted in significant changes to the Dalit condition in colonial and postcolonial India.

Making education accessible for those on the lower rung of society was one of the major steps these Dalit reformers took to empower the Dalits. Phule, the self-taught Dalit reformer, considered education as a tool of social assertion. Moreover, he defied the policy of denying education to women by teaching his wife. She in turn became a social reformer among the Dalit women.

Dalits asserted themselves by adopting upper-caste rituals and even upper-caste gods to subvert upper-caste privileges. For example, Narayana Guru challenged the Brahmanical monopoly on Shiva worship by installing a Shiva idol, which was the exclusive right of Brahmin priests. Shiva was also the god of the upper castes. It was a daring act of religious subversion by a Dalit.

Dalit social reformers were not mere philosophers, but they were pragmatic as well. One of the major contributions of Narayana Guru was to promote industries for the economic uplift of the downtrodden caste he represented.[40]

---

39  Santosh K. Singh, "The Caste Question and Songs of Protest in Punjab," *Economic and Political Weekly* 52, no. 34 (2017).

40  A recent study that highlights the contribution of Sri Narayana Guru is P. Chandramohan, *Developmental Modernity in Kerala: Narayana Guru, S. N. D. P. Yogam, and Social Reform* (New Delhi: Tulika, 2016).

In due time, the colonial rulers picked up the signal that the Dalit assertion movements were sending out. The Government of India Act of 1919 empowered the lower castes to elect their own representatives. This enabled many social reform movements of this period to contest elections and get elected as well. Thus the social movements of the Dalit reformers got a political voice.[41]

Dalits attempted to liberate themselves from the curse of caste by embracing other rather egalitarian faiths. Teltumbde remarks that historically, the Dalits considered religious conversion as a means of emancipation.[42] As part of their struggle for liberation, the Dalits joined different egalitarian faiths, like Kabir Panth and so on. Some, beginning in Moghul times, joined Islam; others joined Christianity.

Besides the mass conversions during the Moghul and European periods, Dalits resorted to mass conversions to liberate themselves from the clutches of Hinduism. Famous among the mass conversions to subvert the power of Hinduism was staged in Meenakshipuram in Tamil Nadu in 1981. In this mass conversion event, 2,600 educated Dalits who had government jobs in this town joined Islam.[43] Such willing conversions are only on the rise in our times.

The creation of a new religious identity through neo-Buddhism is another example of Dalit assertion. Ambedkar initiated himself to neo-Buddhism on October 14, 1956. As Muthaiah explains, "Babasaheb [Ambedkar] gave a class ideology to Dalits through Buddhism which believes in classless and casteless society."[44]

Dalits are not silent sufferers; many instances show that they are capable of organized, sometimes even violent, resistance and assertion of their cause. Among many examples is the case of Dalits in Lathor, a village in Odisha. Dalits here are more educated and employed than those of higher castes in their village. The educated young men among them formed the Krishna Group and created awareness among their members. They chose to stand up to the aggression of the higher castes among them.[45] In order to assert themselves over the upper castes, they refused

41  Barman, "Caste Violence in India," 198.
42  Teltumbde, *Dalits*, 107–18.
43  Sudha Pai, *Dalit Assertion*, 1st ed., Oxford India Short Introductions (New Delhi: Oxford University Press, 2013), 40.
44  Muthaiah, "Politics of Dalit Identity," 397.
45  Khuturam Sunani Nigam, Ranjana Padhi, and Debaranjan Sarangi, "The Price of Dalit Assertion: On the Burning Down of Dalit Houses in Lathore,

to play drums. They found support from the Dalits in other villages as well. They also refused to play drums in the Durga Puja festival, which was traditionally considered their duty as members of the low castes.[46]

In asserting their power, they not only used their might but also used provisions of the law. In the same village, a Dalit woman named Gauri filed a police complaint against the priest who snatched the ritual pot from her. The priest was booked according to the Scheduled Castes and Scheduled Tribes (Prevention of Atrocities) Act of 1989 and sentenced to jail.[47]

The Dalit literature movement was another way to assert their rights. Among many, the documentation by Imtiaz Ahmad and Shashi Bhushan Upadhyay on Dalit assertion through literature is remarkable.[48] Sudha Pai suggests that Dalit assertion has taken on a new expression in the upsurge in Dalit literature in Tamil, which "portrays a new feeling of confidence and fresh thinking on questions of nation, democracy, citizenship, and development."[49] The Dalit literature movement arose in the late 1960s, following in the footsteps of Black literature in the United States that gave expression to their anger. Literary works by Dalit writers have been both assertive and liberative.

Indian independence gave Dalit assertion a new impetus due to increasing democratization and regionalization. In Pai's view, the emergence of the Union of India through its absorption of princely states meant more power to the people who were participants in electoral politics. People had a say in the running of the country and their destiny.[50] The loose federal political system in India facilitates local empowerment, which is conducive to Dalit assertion.

Positive socioeconomic changes since the 1980s have given the Dalits a new confidence and sense of dignity. These changes include a decline in poverty and infant mortality rate, increased public expenditures in rural areas, a doubling of life expectancy, increased literacy, and so on. Pai remarks that "these developments underpinned the rise of Dalit Assertion and revolt against upper caste domination."[51] Surveys have found that

---

OdishaNigam," *Economic and Political Weekly* 47, no. 35 (2012): 19.
46  Nigam, Padhi, and Sarangi, 21.
47  Nigam, Padhi, and Sarangi, 21.
48  Ahmad and Upadhyay, *Dalit Assertion in Society, Literature and History*.
49  Pai, *Dalit Assertion*, 45.
50  Pai, xxix.
51  Pai, xxx.

there have been significant changes in lifestyles, educational levels, and relationships with the upper castes.[52]

Though it may sound ironic, violence against Dalits is evidence of Dalit assertion. One of the reasons for increased violence is Dalits refusing to put up with the oppression of the dominant groups. Instead of suffering atrocities against them, they were fighting back.[53]

There has been significant upward socioeconomic movement among the Dalits. Praveen Chakravarty argues that education and employment levels among Dalits have risen significantly. He quotes an IndiaSpend report from December 13, 2013, to argue that there has been an overall increase of 51 percent in the number of literate persons among the scheduled castes (SCs). However, in urban areas, the literacy rate among the SCs has gone up to 62 percent. According to the same report, the worker participation rate for SCs is 40 percent, which is above the national average of 39.8 percent.[54] He also quotes IndiaSpend's analysis of 2011 census data to point out that Dalit converts (neo-Buddhists) have better literacy rates, higher work participation, and better sex ratios than the SC Hindus.[55] It is obvious that Dalits have made significant progress in all aspects of life over the decades.

Sociologists report that the new market economy and globalization have also lessened the harshness of caste.[56] This is evidenced in the employment patterns that are changing and transcending caste barriers. Education and social advancement have moved Dalits into different socioeconomic categories. On the contrary, as D. Shyam Babu and Chandra Bhan Prasad report, unemployment has driven upper-caste youth into employment in sanitation, which was the traditional occupation of the Dalits.[57]

---

52  Devesh Kapur et al., "Rethinking Inequality: Dalits in Uttar Pradesh in the Market Reform Era," *Economic and Political Weekly* 45, no. 35 (2010): 39–49; Pai, *Dalit Assertion*, 120.

53  Pai, *Dalit Assertion*, 157.

54  Praveen Chakravarty, "Rise of Hindutva Forces, Upper Caste Antagonism Catalyse Drive by Educated Dalits to Assert Their Identity," Firstpost, accessed February 12, 2018, http://www.firstpost.com/india/rise-of-hindutva-forces -upper-caste-antagonism-catalyse-drive-by-educated-dalits-to-assert-their -identity-4335739.html.

55  Chakravarty.

56  D. Shyam Babu and Chandra Bhan Prasad, "Six Dalit Paradoxes," *Economic and Political Weekly* 44, no. 23 (2009): 25.

57  Babu and Prasad, 25.

The reservation policies of independent India were a step that certainly benefited the Dalits and resulted in the emergence of a Dalit middle class. Though the reservation policy goes back as far as 1831 in the Madras Presidency, followed by some "natives states" in the twentieth century, the adoption of the reservation policy for the whole of India took place through the Government of India Act of 1935.[58]

The actions of the British government also facilitated Dalit political power. The Simon Commission of 1927 and the Round Table Conferences of 1930–32 leading to the Government of India Act of 1935 resulted in the growth of political consciousness among the lower castes.[59] The British decision of a separate electorate for the lower castes was a step toward empowering the lower castes, but it was opposed by Mahatma Gandhi. But it did not see the light of day, as Gandhi and B. R. Ambedkar reached an agreement resulting in the Poona Pact in 1932.

After colonialism, the Constitution of India also guaranteed protection of the rights of every individual, including the Dalits. Clause 4 of article 15 made a provision for the advancement of backward classes, and article 16 extended these privileges to public employment for the backward classes.[60]

Many other acts of the Indian government furthered the Dalit emergence. Prominent among them are the Mandal Commission of 1979–80, which recommended 27 percent of seats in admission to academic institutions and government jobs. The Untouchability Practices Act (1955), the Scheduled Castes and Scheduled Tribes (Prevention of Atrocities) Act (1989), and so on that provided Dalits dignity.

The increased confidence in their power has led the Dalits to assert themselves using sociopolitical and cultural symbols. Visitors to government offices, particularly those in Maharashtra, cannot escape noticing the bust or framed photographs of Ambedkar, the Dalit icon, installed in prominent places and venerated daily. Besides the installation of statues of Ambedkar in public places, schools and institutions are named after him all over India.

Another manifestation of Dalit power is in social and cultural spaces through the formation of Dalit organizations and Dalit activism. These are clusters of Dalit power and presence led by educated Dalit

---

58  Barman, "Caste Violence in India," 199.
59  Barman, 198.
60  Barman, 199–200.

lawyers, teachers, and intellectuals.[61] The new Dalit middle class, also known as the "creamy layer" in the Dalit communities, has emerged through the favorable policies of the state and can be seen in various aspects of Indian life.

The new Dalit middle class is expressing its power through Dalit parties and electoral politics. Dalit-based parties aim to capture power through the electoral process. Historically, they were mere vote banks for mainline parties like the Indian National Congress. It is true that the Dalit emergence in politics is partly due to the changed attitude of upper-caste politicians toward Dalits. Since the 1920s, there have been significant changes in the attitudes of upper-caste politicians toward caste practices. The temple entry campaigns for the untouchables led by M. K. Gandhi are examples of the fight for the rights of the Dalits. The Indian National Congress, under the leadership of M. K. Gandhi and other politicians, changed their attitude toward the Dalits. In his in-depth study of Indian politics since independence, Christophe Jaffrelot concludes that "India is therefore experimenting with a silent revolution. Power is being transferred, on the whole peacefully, from the upper caste elites to various subaltern groups."[62]

Another important form of Dalit assertion in postindependent India is Dalit middle-class activism.[63] According to Pai, this new form of assertion began in the 1990s, ushered in by "a small, better educated, influential, and younger generation Dalit middle class."[64]

One facet of Dalit middle-class activism is aimed at enhancing opportunities for Dalits where there is no state involvement. The reservation policy has only created a small group of educated government employees among the Dalits. This middle class has an English education, and they are situated in the senior ranks of Indian bureaucracy as the result of the preferential treatment guaranteed by the Indian Constitution. But the Dalits are kept out of business, technology, industry, and so on in the private sector. Damodaran has found that there are practically no significant Dalit industrialists in India.[65]

---

61  Pai, *Dalit Assertion*, 38.

62  Christophe Jaffrelot, *India's Silent Revolution: The Rise of the Lower Castes in North Indian Politics* (Delhi: Permanent Black, 2003), 494.

63  Pai, *Dalit Assertion*, 116–49.

64  Pai, 116.

65  Harish Damodaran, *India's New Capitalists: Caste, Business, and Industry in a Modern Nation-State* (New Delhi: Permanent Black, 2008).

The efforts of the new Dalit middle class, demanding equality and doing advocacy for their unprivileged Dalit comrades, have resulted in the formulation of the Bhopal Document (BD) and the Dalit Agenda.[66] Various governments have implemented the BD policy since 2002 under different schemes. This has resulted in the emergence of a new entrepreneurial class of Dalits in Madhya Pradesh, where this was implemented by the government led by Chief Minister Digvijay Singh. As Teltumbde points out, this government drew up a plan of "producing at least 5,000 entrepreneurs belonging to [the] Dalits/tribals category every year and 25,000 entrepreneurs in five years."[67]

Not only is the Bhopal initiative attempting to involve Dalits in various economic ventures, but other agencies have been formed to give the Dalits a place in India's economic life. The Dalit Indian Chamber of Commerce and Industry (DICCI), formed in 2005, is one of them. Teltumbde reports that many business leaders, like Ratan Tata, Adi Godrej, and others, have given visible support to this initiative by attending DICCI conferences.[68] DICCI's tagline is "Be job-givers—not job seekers!" These initiatives of the Dalit middle class are certainly ambitious, but being rather new, their impact is still to be seen. However, they provide significant evidence that the Dalits in the independent era have evolved to be a people of power, rich in imagination and empathy for their own.

## Conclusion

We have seen that the word *Dalit* carries two contrasting nuances of pathos and power. This duality of the word's meaning is also attested by Dalit history, which is a combination of suffering as well as the assertion of power. Their past and present provide evidence of undeniable violence against them and the derision with which they are treated. At the same time, history testifies that they are a people with immense power to affirm and assert themselves and others. Though they are objects of both injustice and violence, they are also people of great potential, as evidenced in

---

66  Pai, *Dalit Assertion*, 122.
67  Teltumbde, *Dalits*, 148.
68  Teltumbde, 149.

their historical roles as rulers, freedom fighters, ingenious discoverers, and leaders of reform movements.

These facts lead all those who aspire for integral transformation to harness the power of the subalterns to better human life. Power as well as pathos should be concerns of the theologian; in the case of the subalterns, it is crucial to tap their proven, inherent power to alleviate their pathos.

# PART II

## The Way Forward

# 5

---

# ENGAGEMENTS FOR
# SOCIAL TRANSFORMATION

Dalit liberation theology has run its course. As some scholars have pointed out, its theological efficacy remains questioned. Its impact on society and the church is also minimal. This could be due to limitations in its hermeneutical methodology, the partial perception of the Dalit reality, and other reasons.

However, the theological task in India is not limited to liberating one section of the population from one aspect of their disadvantages. The theological task should have larger goals that embrace the entire society and should be integral, touching all aspects of human life.

We also note that the subalterns, including the Dalits, are emerging as a powerful force in newly independent India. In the next section of this book, with the benefit of hindsight, I suggest some ways in which the church in India can undertake its task to bring out radical changes in society, bringing the kingdom of God into the life of India.

I begin this section with two case studies where Christian witnesses are engaged in social transformation. The history of the engagement of the Christian gospel to fight social evils should inform the present and future.

The first case study is one in which the Christian gospel successfully confronted a social evil in Indian society—the abolition of sati. The other is a case where the gospel message failed miserably in eradicating the evil of caste in the Indian churches, where it had absolute control. These two case studies give us important leads to reflect on future engagement for integral transformation.

At the very outset, we should note that education is the very foundation for the transformation of any society. In India, education beyond the
boundaries of gender and caste was possible through educational institutions that the Christian missionaries established all over the country.
Most of the towering political figures, social thinkers, and reformers of
modern India are the products of these institutions. We also need to recognize that the Christian presence and witness in India have impacted
society directly and indirectly in various other ways. However, here we
focus on two specific cases where the Christian church, largely the product of colonial rule, engaged in fighting social evils.

## Case 1: Abolition of Sati

The abolition of the rite of sati is one of the many social evils that the
Christian gospel directly impacted. Sati is the practice of immolating
the widow on the funeral pyre of her deceased husband. Some segments
of Hindu society glorified sati as an act of devotion, holiness, virtue,
and so on. In some cases, memorials were built for those women who
dared to offer their bodies to be burned.[1] Sati was widespread in India
from north to south. However, the highest number of incidents of sati
were recorded in the Bengal Presidency of the British raj.

Sati was an age-old social evil in India that went unchallenged until
European missionaries came on the scene. Historical records of sati go
back to the fourth century BCE, but condemning the practice and campaigning to abolish it happened only after the arrival of Christian missionaries. Arvind Sharma points out that during the period from the fourth
century BCE to 1757, reactions to sati were a mix of both admiration
and criticism. But during the period between 1757 and 1857, Christian
missionaries were actively involved in condemning the practice, which
led to its abolition in 1829.[2]

The abolition of sati in 1829 is the culmination of the campaigns
of many European missionaries, particularly the Serampore trio, led by
William Carey. Sharma points out that they campaigned against this evil

---

1 For photographs of inscriptions and monuments related to sati, see Meenakshi
   Jain, *Sati: Evangelicals, Baptist Missionaries, and the Changing Colonial Discourse*
   (New Delhi: Aryan Books International, 2016).
2 Arvind Sharma, "Sati: A Study in Western Reactions," in *Sati: Historical and
   Phenomenological Essays*, ed. Arvind Sharma, 1st ed. (Delhi: Motilal Banarsidass,
   1988), 1–13.

because they witnessed at least one actual instance of this practice where the victim was forced directly or indirectly to immolate herself.[3]

The Christian campaign against sati was multifaceted. The missionaries directed their campaign at the victims, the perpetrators, the government, the public, and Hindu intellectuals. Ajit Ray cites an incident where Carey visited a site where a sati was about to be performed. He tried to convince the widow and the priests who were going to perform the rite to stop the ceremony. However, he was not successful, since they insisted that it was not an act of "shocking murder," as Carey argued, but "an act of holiness."[4] In another incident cited by Meenakshi Jain, Carey attempted to frighten a group planning a sati by saying that the governor-general had ordered that the first person to light the pyre would be hanged.[5]

Carey's campaign against sati involved collecting data to be presented to government authorities. He sent out people to collect data about widow immolation in a thirty-mile radius of Calcutta in one year. This is the area where the Baptist missionaries worked. The researchers found that there were 438 cases of sati in one year in the area of their research. The data were not just counting the victims, but as Jain points out, they included the ages of the victims and the number of children they left behind.[6] The missionaries included these details to spotlight the inhumanness and cruelty of this evil.

These data were used to raise public opinion against sati in India and Britain. Ray points out that Wilberforce cited the statistics published by Carey and his colleagues in the House of Commons on June 22, 1813. To persuade the house, he included in his speech an eyewitness account by Joshua Marshman.[7] The Christians who campaigned against sati moved the government machinery against it. In their campaign against sati, the Serampore trio wrote letters to the government citing the data they had collected.[8]

The campaign was also through means of journalism. In 1823, the Serampore missionaries published a collection of essays, of which the first

3 Sharma, 7.

4 Ajit Ray, "Widows Are Not for Burning: Christian Missionary Participation in the Abolition of the Sati Rite," in Sharma, Sati, 58.

5 Jain, Sati, 178.

6 Jain, 180.

7 Jain has cited this horrific case as Wilberforce narrated. See Jain, 184.

8 Sharma, "Sati," 7.

three were fierce attacks on sati. Unnamed missionaries were also involved in campaigning against sati. As Sharma records, in 1827, an anonymous work attacking sati was published by a missionary.[9] Many other missionaries were involved in the campaign against sati through their publications and educated the lawmakers in Britain. The Christian missionaries used the publications that they started during this period. For example, as Jain points out, the quarterly magazine that Marshman founded in 1818 published a series of articles during 1822–23 opposing sati.[10] These articles were republished in Britain subsequently to educate the colonial rulers. The Christian missionaries also created awareness against sati through various books, pamphlets, and so on.

Raja Rammohun Ray, who was influenced by the Serampore trio, also campaigned against sati. Sharma notes that Ray "launched his journalistic attack" on sati, ignoring the threat to his life, in 1818. He also published a tract against sati in 1821.[11] These publications through periodicals, books, and pamphlets had wider repercussions. For example, the January–March 1826 issue of the *Oriental Herald and the Journal of General Literature* carried a twenty-page article on widow immolation.[12] Thus the journalistic work of the missionaries had a wider academic impact that marshaled the opinion of intellectuals against sati. Ray says, "Stirred by the public interest which the missionaries had aroused by their publicity, and anxious to terminate the rite without causing much unrest among the Hindus, the Parliament, the Board of Control, and the British people became more concerned with the issue."[13]

The campaign against sati was also addressed to the non-Christian public. The Christian missionaries also influenced many Hindu leaders to support the abolition of sati. Thus, though the Hindu opinion was not united against sati, this helped Hindu opinion swing in favor of abolition. Among the most prominent of such scholars was Mrtyunjaya Vidyalankara, a Brahmin scholar. In 1817, he declared that sati had no sanction in Hindu law. His position helped in the formation of Hindu opinion against sati. This scholar was a "friend and colleague of William Carey" as well as his teacher.[14] He was very sympathetic to Carey's concern about

---

9 Sharma, 7.
10 Jain, *Sati*, 196.
11 Sharma, "Sati," 7.
12 Jain, *Sati*, 197.
13 Ray, "Widows Are Not for Burning," 61.
14 Ray, 63.

sati. Roy, who also paraded against sati, used this scholar's interpretations in his campaigns against sati.

Secular historians claim that the missionaries achieved something that society had accommodated and the state tried to ignore. Ray comments, "The abolition of the sati rite in 1829 owes much to the efforts of the Christian missionaries. Under the watchful eye of a Government which was hesitant to take any action to terminate the rite, and reluctant to allow the missionary interference in the religious beliefs of the native, and in the face of rather cold indifference of the native people, the missionaries started working for the abolition of a practice which they thought inhuman."[15]

It must be noted that while the evangelicals and Baptist missionaries were actively engaged in the campaign against sati, the Catholics and Anglicans were apparently passive. We have no historical information about the Catholic reaction to sati. Historians have noted that Bishop Heber, who was the Anglican bishop in Calcutta during the height of the campaign against sati, took only an academic interest in the issue and did not join the Baptist missionaries of Calcutta in their efforts. Ray remarks that "Reginald Heber, the second Protestant Bishop of Calcutta, was concerned with the burning of the widows, but he took a rather academic interest in the subject."[16] Though he had witnessed a funeral pyre immediately after the immolation, his interest was in the position of the widow on the pyre and details of the rite. Instead of becoming involved in the campaign against sati, he thought that as education became more widespread through Christian schools, sati would come to an end on its own.[17]

## Case 2: The Battle against Caste in the Church

Caste in the Indian society is something that the church in India did not challenge but rather accommodated. The history of caste in the church and the church's toleration of it speaks volumes about the culpability of the church in India and its social irresponsibility. The Indian church failed to be an agent of liberation on two fronts regarding the caste system, which is the root of all social evils and inequalities in Indian society. First, it failed in its obligation to be an agent of transformation to fight this evil

---

15  Ray, 62.
16  Ray, 59.
17  Ray, 60.

in society, unlike non-Christian social reformers like Phule, Ambedkar, Gandhi, and others. Second, it also failed to eliminate caste practices within its own walls, failing miserably in providing justice, equality, and dignity to converts from lower castes who came under its wings.

Before the European missionary enterprise in India, the Indian church, being homogeneous, was rather immune to caste discrimination. For example, the ancient Christians of the present Kerala state were accorded the status of "high caste" by the local rulers. Since this Christian community was endogamous and less zealous in its missionary activity, it did not have to face the issues of caste. In a similar manner, the Roman Catholic mission before the arrival of Roberto de Nobili (1577–1656) was exclusively among the fishermen. So caste discrimination was not an issue for the churches.

Caste issues raised their ugly head when the church became heterogeneous as conversions through European missionary efforts began. The European missions converted people from various lower as well as higher castes, resulting in heterogeneous churches. The missionary churches were either exclusively among the lower castes or in mixed groups where high-caste Christians dominated. Wherever two different castes came into close proximity as members of the same congregation, caste discrimination showed up.

Since the mixed congregations were hindrances to conversion from high castes, the European missionaries tried to accommodate the caste sensitivities of the local people. One method was inculturation by adapting high-caste practices in the church to make the Christian faith acceptable to the high castes. The second issues from the first by segregating the congregations according to caste to maintain homogeneity.

The pioneer of the inculturation method is indisputably Roberto de Nobili, who adapted Hindu customs to reach out to high-caste Hindus. Upon his arrival as a missionary in India in 1605, he realized that the high-caste Hindus considered the Portuguese customs offensive.[18] In order to make Christianity more acceptable to high-caste Hindus, he introduced caste practices into the church. In the process, he identified himself with the Brahmins and practiced caste by dissociating with the lower castes. Though de Nobili was uncompromising on doctrinal matters, he allowed the high-caste converts to maintain their social practices.[19]

---

**18** J. L. Brockington, *Hinduism and Christianity* (New York: Springer, 2016), 168.
**19** Brockington, 169.

De Nobili's mission in Madurai promoted the idea of separate churches for separate castes to keep the low castes away from the high-caste converts. He was keen to keep the congregations homogeneous to avoid caste conflicts.

The Catholic Church reproduced caste structures within itself. Ashok Kumar opines that the Catholic Church, by its very nature tolerant and accommodating toward caste in India, perpetuated the caste system within itself. Kumar points out that this policy made the lower castes feel extremely uncomfortable with the church.[20]

Even the non-Catholic missions followed de Nobili's model by having separate churches and seating places according to caste. As Charles Hoole rightly points out, Christian Friederich Schwartz (1726–98) of the Tranquebar Mission toed the de Nobili line, which had influenced the churches and missions in the southern part of India. This had very negative consequences as well. As Hoole argues, "Owing to this policy of tolerance, Anglican churches in Vepery, Trichinopoly and Tanjore by the beginning of the nineteenth century had become indisciplined, corrupt, riven with internal conflicts and experienced a steady flow of reversions to Hinduism."[21]

In fact, early European missionaries of the colonial era did not fully understand the evils of the caste system. They might have taken it to be a social or religious custom, like the social divides they were familiar with in their countries of origin.[22] However, when the Christian missions realized that caste and caste discrimination were against the Christian ethos, they did fight against such evil practices, particularly in the churches. However, it took more than two hundred years after the arrival of the first European missionary for them to realize that caste is an evil system and not a passive social practice. Though late, when this awareness dawned on the church, it did fight caste discrimination within the fold.

---

20  Ashok Kumar M., "Dalits Preaching to Dalits: Lutheran Modes of Combating Caste Marginality in Andhra, South India," *Indian Anthropologist* 45, no. 1 (2015): 65–66.

21  Charles Hoole, "Bishop Wilson and the Origins of Dalit Liberation," *Transformation* 21, no. 1 (2004): 42.

22  Christopher, "Between Two Worlds," 17.

## The Lost Battle against Caste: Roman Catholics

We should note that long before the organized campaign against caste in the churches began, the leadership of the Roman Catholic Church raised objections as early as the first part of the seventeenth century. Though Pope Gregory XV approved de Nobili's mission approach through his constitution *Romanae Sedis Antistes*, issued on January 31, 1623, he exhorted the high-caste Hindu converts to stop practicing caste in the church. However, this was ignored, and caste practices continued.

The Catholic bishop of Myalapore attempted to cleanse the churches of caste discrimination in 1921, asking the Indian hierarchy to implement the terms of the Propaganda Fide of 1783. This required them to abolish the practice of allowing separate seats in the churches according to caste status. But both leaders and laity opposed this move. His attempts to implement the Propaganda Fide of 1865, which demanded that all castes must be admitted to schools, also were opposed by the high-caste Christians. Though the South Indian bishops wrote a common pastoral letter in 1933 advocating the abolition of caste distinction in the church, it could not be implemented, as it was met with severe opposition from leaders and laity alike.[23] Prakash Louis also points out that though the Synod of Pondicherry in 1844 issued a statement against allotting seats according to castes, the Christians from high castes opposed it by boycotting the churches until the order was revoked.[24]

Besides these attempts, the Roman Catholic Church did little to oppose caste. It believed in accommodation rather than challenging the social order. Moreover, as Christopher notes, the Vatican's emphasis on indigenization allowed native elements, including caste, to be tolerated by the church so that the Dalits were denied equality with others.[25]

---

23   L. Stanislaus, *The Liberative Mission of the Church among Dalit Christians* (New Delhi: ISPCK, 1999). Referred to by Prakash Louis, "Dalit Christians: Betrayed by State and Church," *Economic and Political Weekly* 42, no. 16 (2007): 1405.

24   Louis, "Dalit Christians," 1405.

25   Christopher, "Between Two Worlds," 17–18.

## The Lost Battle against Caste: Non-Catholic Battlefront

Though initially, the European non-Catholic missionaries in India did not realize the evils of caste and ignored it as a social practice unique to India, the scene changed over two centuries of engagement with India.

The Anglican bishops Reginald Heber and his successor, Daniel Wilson, are two notable figures in the battle against the evils of caste. Heber (1783–1826) was bishop of Calcutta (present-day Kolkata) for a short period of three years, from 1823 until his death in 1826 in Tiruchirappalli.[26] Heavily distressed by the evil of caste, he set out on a tour of the southern part of India on January 30, 1826, to study the issue of caste in the churches.

On March 21, 1826, within three months of his arrival in Tamil Nadu in the southern part of India, he ordered an inquiry into the caste question in the churches under his jurisdiction. Bishop Heber was not fortunate enough to see the outcome of the study, since he died two weeks after he ordered it.[27] However, the last sermon that he preached on the day of his death in Trichinopoly (present-day Trichy) was against the caste system.

But Bishop Heber's efforts were not in vain. The study he ordered continued despite his death, leading to the united opinion of various denominations in present-day India and Sri Lanka (Ceylon) against caste practices in the churches. All Protestant churches except the Danish Mission were against maintaining caste in the Protestant churches.[28] In spite of this united opinion of the European mission organizations, caste stayed on to confront another challenger who was determined to exorcise it from the Indian Christian church. That was Bishop Daniel Wilson of Calcutta.

His association with social reformers like William Wilberforce and John Newton (1725–1807), who fought against slavery in Britain, had convinced Bishop Wilson that the Christian gospel had a role to play in social transformation. We have already noted his theological reflections on social evils. When he was appointed bishop in India, he continued the fight against social evils—the only difference was the

---

26 During this time, the whole of British India and Sri Lanka (Ceylon) were under the bishoprics of Calcutta.

27 Bateman, *Daniel Wilson*, 235.

28 Bateman, 236.

battlefield and the enemy. His new battlefield was colonial India, and the new enemy was the caste system in the churches that was now two centuries old.

Wilson realized that all that he had to do was to implement the consensus that the leadership of the different churches had arrived at as the result of the fruitful labor of his predecessor. His approach is known as the "Wilson line." As the great crusader against the social evil of caste in India, he followed the trail of his predecessor, Bishop Heber, by taking the long journey to the southern states, where caste discrimination reigned in the churches. He was determined to force his ideology of human dignity and equality on the congregations under his jurisdiction.

Wilson used whatever power he had at his disposal as the head of the Anglican Church in India. His letters came with dire warnings. He threatened disciplinary actions against church officials who practiced caste in the churches under his jurisdiction.[29]

Wilson was very practical in his attempt to eliminate caste practices from the church. Besides writing letters banning caste practices in the churches under his care, he visited the churches and preached against caste. He got personally involved in the action. During his visit to Trichinopoly, he was able to reconcile the congregation by personally persuading them. He went and greeted the people of the Soodra caste who were standing aloof from the lower castes and personally brought them to sit together, holding hands.[30] This intermingled service was repeated in many places where he went.

Though there were many nonconformists, Bishop Wilson was confident that the little yeast that would leaven the whole lump was formed. "A nucleus is now formed," he wrote, "as I hope, in all the stations for a sound and permanent Christian doctrine and discipline."[31] Wilson hoped that this nucleus would eventually effect a great transformation. But history shows that his hopes were not realized.

Wilson's effort to eradicate caste discrimination and reconcile the castes was only partial and temporary. Though under pressure and persuasion there was a visible reconciliation through seating arrangements and participation in the bishop's presence, the changes did not last long. The converts to Christianity from various castes opposed his efforts

---

29  Bateman, 239, citing a letter dated July 5, 1833.
30  Bateman, 257.
31  Bateman, 260.

vehemently. The revolt against Bishop Wilson's decision almost led to a split. His biographer later recorded that "seventeen hundred soodras had withdrawn from public worship, and never came near the church."[32] The rebels formed parallel congregations, where they appointed their own priests. They also opened a school for the children of the Soodra caste. Josiah Bateman also records that this bitter reaction to the "Wilson Line" made the European missionaries very unpopular among some sections of the church in those regions.[33]

The revolt against his attempts at reform broke Bishop Wilson's heart. His anguish and distress during this period are evident in his journals. During his visit to Madras (Chennai) in 1835 during the revolt against his decision, he penned this prayer in his journal: "To thee do I look up. As to myself and human power, my heart faileth me. For what can I do with seventeen hundred revolters, and ten thousand uninformed and prejudiced Christians? Lord, undertake for me."[34]

Wilberforce succeeded in eradicating slavery from Britain, but Bishop Wilson, his close friend and companion engaged in the same mission with him in his country, failed to do the same in the Indian church, over which he had absolute control. Bishops Heber, Wilson, and many other unsung enthusiasts must be commended for their labor to bring about social transformation in the Indian church, at least in caste discrimination. Despite their honest and sincere efforts, caste-based discrimination continues in the Indian churches.

## Lessons from the Case Studies

What are we to learn from these two case studies that present us with two models of the gospel engaging with society?

First, two contrasting views on mission are evident here. One focuses on church expansion and the other on social transformation, disregarding the gains of expansion. Bishop Wilson came to realize that caste was destroying the Christian witness and mission, particularly in southern India. Wilson's biographer Bateman reports that 168 converts had gone back to Hinduism in one year because of the caste discrimination they

32  Bateman, 247.
33  Bateman, 247.
34  Bateman, 247.

encountered in the churches.[35] Hoole remarks that Wilson "was convinced that the retention of caste customs among Christians was not only a scandal to their religion, but also provided a convenient bridge which increasing numbers were now using to return to their previous faith. In short retention of caste encouraged apostasy."[36] The same thing can be said about the Catholics who encouraged accommodation as a policy of expansionism.

However, the Serampore missionaries had no such goals. Their sole aim was to transform Indian society forever and to secure the future of widows. They were aiming not at church growth but at the growth of the kingdom of God into all areas of human existence. Their focus was social transformation.

The missionaries involved in the campaign against sati were convinced that the gospel belonged to the public square. This conviction led the campaigners against sati to address the wider public: the potential victims and collaborators like priests, politicians, and the public. Bishops Heber and Wilson were solely concerned about the church in their care. The Anglican hierarchy limited themselves to their flock, exhorting and even threatening them to stop the practice.

These case studies also show the importance of empowered individuals in integral transformation. The campaign against sati concluded successfully because it was led by informed individuals. They were empowered by the conviction that a practice like sati is inhuman, contrary to the values of any religion, and violates the rights and dignity of human beings. The fight against caste practices within the church failed miserably because the individuals were not transformed by the gospel. As we have seen in the previous chapters, Wilson wrote against caste practices in strong language, even employing biblical metaphors. Wilson's sincere attempts were thwarted by the high castes, who not only opposed his policies but also led to a split in the church. In a similar way, the attempts of the Catholic hierarchies were also defeated by the people themselves. Integral transformation depends on the participation of empowered individuals. The transformative power of the gospel is invested not in the power of the hierarchy but in the conscience of the empowered individuals. In the fight against caste in the churches, the people rejected everything that the hierarchy dictated. However, in the case

---

35  Bateman, 237.
36  Hoole, "Bishop Wilson," 42.

of sati, the campaigners ensured that abolition was the agenda of the people as well.

The fight against caste was a duel between two structures in which the strongest prevailed. The fight against sati was not a conflict of structure but the permeation of the gospel into all strata of society. The battle against caste in the churches that European missionaries fought was against the church structure, modeled after Constantine's empire, another age-old social structure erected to protect the interests of the social elite in India. The caste system had prevailed in many assaults against it from its very inception, which had helped it develop immunity. And in this battle too, it prevailed.

Two important themes emerge from these studies. First, they challenge us to imagine church in new ways. Being the agent of God's transformation, it is important to rethink its nature and mission in the contemporary world. The second has to do with the public relevance of the Christian faith. I would like to explore these concerns further in the following chapters to make Christian theology in India put out its sails and surge beyond the lull to transform its context in God's ways.

# 6

# REIMAGINING
# THE CHURCH

Imagination will often carry us to worlds that never were, but
without it we go nowhere.

—Carl Sagan

As noted earlier, critics have suggested that Dalit liberation theology
maintains a Christology that is inadequate for Dalit liberation. Moreover, it also lacks a pneumatology. Besides these major lapses, the inad-
equacy of its ecclesiology has been under fire from its critics as well as
its practitioners. What Eugene Baron and Moses Maponya recognized
as the need for the church in South Africa is true of the church in India
too. They argue that for the church to become more prophetic, church
members need to be encouraged to reimagine the nature of the church.[1]
The reimagining of the church in the following pages will intertwine the
otherwise ignored themes of Christology and pneumatology.

There are many reasons that compel us to reimagine the church in
India besides the observation that an ecclesiology that enables integral
transformation is lacking in Dalit liberation theology. We have already
seen that Dalit Christians and scholars have demanded that the very
structure and practices of the church need to be transformed. Moreover, the churches in the Global South, including India, are increasingly

---

1 Eugene Baron and Moses Maponya, "The Recovery of the Prophetic Voice of the
Church: The Adoption of a 'Missional Church' Imagination," *Verbum et Ecclesia*
41, no. 1 (July 27, 2020): 5.

independent of the Western missions in their modes of thinking, especially in ecclesiology.

As Christianity is shifting to the Global South, there is a great demand for the church to be imagined not as an extension of Western ecclesiastical structures but as a community of believers. In India, Christian faith is finding new expressions independent of the West, especially in being the church of Jesus Christ. Among the many modern writers who have discerned this hunger of the new churches in the Global South is Miroslav Volf. He says, "In many churches, especially those of the non-Western world, this desire is quite robust. I would like to provide these churches with the ecclesiological categories through which they might better understand themselves as and live better as a community."[2] John W. Stewart endorses Volf, saying that "few can doubt, however, the bar is raised in the current discourse about ecclesiology."[3] There is a huge array of ecclesiological models in contemporary theological discourse.[4] However, our purpose is to narrow our search to a model that has the Global South in view and has the potential for integral transformation. In the following pages, I will be drawing on the model of ecclesiology that Volf developed with a view toward the emerging churches in the non-Western world, which in my opinion has the potential to marshal the Indian church to its mission of integral transformation.

## Church Defined

The church should not be imagined merely as physical or a power structure; on the contrary, church is essentially the community gathered in Jesus's name. Volf follows the long tradition of church fathers—for example, Ignatius, Tertullian, and others—to find the definition of the church in Matthew 18:20. He affirms that "where two or three are gathered in Christ's name, not only is Christ present among them, but a Christian

2  Miroslav Volf, *After Our Likeness: The Church as the Image of the Trinity*, Sacra Doctrina (Grand Rapids, MI: Eerdmans, 1997), 11.

3  John W. Stewart, "The Shape of the Church: Congregational and Trinitarian," *Christian Century*, May 20, 1998, 542.

4  For a spectrum of models and debates on ecclesiology, see Kärkkäinen Veli-Matti, *An Introduction to Ecclesiology. Historical, Global, and Interreligious Perspectives*, rev. ed. (Downers Grove, IL: IVP Academic, 2021).

church is there as well, perhaps a bad church, a church that may well transgress against love and truth, but a church nonetheless."[5]

Though church is the gathering of people, not all gatherings are qualified to be a church. However, the gathering should be in Christ's name, as Volf asserts: "Gathering in the name of Christ is the precondition for the presence of Christ in the Holy Spirit, which is itself constitutive for the church."[6] This means that those who are gathered are committed to allowing Christ to determine their lives.[7] He further rivets his argument by saying that "without an acknowledgment of Christ as Lord, there is no church."[8]

## The Mission of Jesus

This commitment of the gathered community to Christ determines its mission as well. Ecclesiology should be rooted in the transforming mission of Jesus Christ. Jesus's sense of being sent by the Father God for the mission of God is clear in the Nazareth Manifesto (Luke 4:16–21). In this exposition of the Old Testament passages, Jesus also declared that his mission is to accomplish a broad spectrum of transformation that involves physical healing, deliverance from exploitation, and freedom from oppression.

True to this self-understanding, Jesus challenged the social, economic, racial, and political boundaries in his ministry. He affirmed the poor while condemning the rich (Luke 6:24). But the poor and the rich had equal access to him, as he pulled down the barriers that divided them. In the community he built, the poor fishermen and rich people like Simon the leper feasted together (Mark 14:3–9). A woman could walk into such a get-together to touch Jesus's feet. Though he himself paid the Roman tax (Matt 17:27), he challenged the tax collectors who oppressed the poor. That was done not by protesting the tax system but by the transformation of tax collectors like Levi (Mark 2:13–17) who followed him and the conversion of Zacchaeus (Luke 19:1–8). By transforming the tax collectors, he debunked the exploitative Roman tax system. He insisted on distributing wealth when he challenged the rich ruler to sell all that he had and give to the poor (Mark 10:21; Luke 18:22). He held

---

5 Volf, *After Our Likeness*, 136.
6 Volf, 145.
7 Volf, 147.
8 Volf, 148.

that wealth is not for hoarding but must be used for the welfare of society. The transformation of Jesus was integral, as it liberated the disadvantaged and transformed the oppressors to abhor their evil ways.

## The Early Church in Christ's Mission

Christ Jesus sent the church to continue his ministry of integral transformation for which the Father God had sent him. A significant shift in mission thinking happened in 1966 at the Berlin World Congress on Evangelism. Samuel Escobar points out that in that conference, John Stott "shifted our attention from the classic passages of Matthew 28:18–20 to the almost forgotten text of the Commission in John 20:21, 'As the Father has sent me, I am sending you.'"[9] Escobar says that here we have not only a mandate for mission but a model for our mission. This passage in John emphasizes that the church has the mandate to continue the mission of Jesus Christ exactly the way he did it in obedience to the Father God who sent him.

The early church and the apostles continued the mission of the Father God that Jesus modeled. They were inspired by their understanding that Jesus, the Messiah sent by God, is the one who has sent them.

Though they were socially and politically insignificant people, the early church believed that Jesus is the Christ who put them in charge of the world they lived in. They challenged the systems that governed their world, since they believed that Christ is the victor, and he reigns. Their conviction that Jesus the Messiah has taken over stimulated their mission. In Pauline thinking, as Delano Palmer and Dieumeme Noelliste put it, "the Messiah is still large and in charge of Empire, for 'he must reign until he has put his enemies under his feet' (1 Cor 15:25)."[10] In other words, Paul argues that the Messiah has taken over the empire. He has begun subjugating the evil systems that will culminate in total annihilation in the future. Though there is a tension in the present and the not yet, Christ is powerful and present in the struggles of the oppressed of the world.

---

9  Samuel Escobar, *A Time for Mission: The Challenge for Global Christianity* (Carlisle, UK: Langham Global Library, 2013), 12.

10  Delano Palmer and Dieumeme Noelliste, "Christ and Liberation: Toward a Messianic Christology for a Postcolonial Society," in *Diverse and Creative Voices: Theological Essays from the Majority World*, ed. Sung Wook Chung and Dieumeme Noelliste (Havertown, UK: James Clarke, 2015), 91.

This conviction of the apostles led them to build interracial and interclass communities where they practiced mutual sharing, or koinonia, all over the Greco-Roman world. One evident example is the list of noteworthy people in the church in Rome, which is a mixture of Greek and Jewish names (Rom 16:3–16). Further evidence of mutual sharing and caring comes from the Christian community in Jerusalem, where the poor and needy were cared for, which again was a racially mixed group (Acts 2:44–45; 4:34–35; 6:1–6). Good works and charity were the virtues they promoted (Acts 9:36–39; 11:28–30). They valued sharing with others more than receiving (Acts 20:35). This is not limited to communities that Peter or Paul initiated; James also believed that the Christian message directly addresses human issues. As Palmer and Noelliste put it, true faith for James is "a philanthropic engagement with especially the poor."[11] We can thus conclude that engagement with the poor in the early church was not limited to any communities and was the hallmark of the Christian church.

The concern for the poor that they exhibited was not limited to their localities or to their own race, but it crossed all imaginable boundaries of race, gender, and class. Paul raised funds from all over Asia and Europe for the poor, suffering Jewish Christians in Jerusalem (Rom 15:25–28; 1 Cor 16:1–4). The Jerusalem community absorbed the widows to be cared for (Acts 6:1; 9:39; 1 Tim 5:3; James 1:27). The community that met in Philemon's house was told to accept a runaway slave called Onesimus and treat him as a brother (Phlm 1:16), according him equality and dignity.

They had a vision for those who were on the margins of society. As Byron Williams says, "A community that cannot see those on the margins is an ecclesia that is inconsistent with the teachings of Jesus."[12] The early church did not limit its vision to caring for the poor, but as Lopez points out from the book of James, they maintained the "prophetic criticism of those who oppressed them."[13] See James 2:1–26 and 5:1–6, where we see James reproaching the wealthy.

---

11  Palmer and Noelliste, 100.

12  Byron Williams, "Prophetic Public Theology," *Review & Expositor* 111, no. 2 (May 2014): 165.

13  Dario Lopez, "The Church as Liberated and Liberating Community: A Primer for a Latin American Ecclesiology," in Chung and Noelliste, *Diverse and Creative Voices*, 165.

## The Holy Spirit in Transforming Mission

Besides the direct link with Christ's mission, the church also recognized that the power for mission comes from the same source—the Holy Spirit that empowered Jesus was the same Holy Spirit that empowered them.

Jesus and the early church were engaged in a mission of liberation in the power of the Holy Spirit. Luke presents Jesus's ministry to the poor and the marginalized as a mission of liberation in the power of the Holy Spirit. Luke affirms that Jesus was "full of the Holy Spirit" after his baptism (Luke 4:1). When he announced his plan of action, he claimed, "The Spirit of the Lord is upon me" (Luke 4:18). Above all, even his incarnation was the work of the Holy Spirit, as the Holy Spirit came upon Mary and the power of the Most High overshadowed her (Luke 1:35).

The centrality of the Spirit in the life and mission of Christ is also evident in the church. It is the Holy Spirit that constituted the church in the Upper Room on the day of Pentecost. The power of the Holy Spirit was transferred to the community of the disciples on the day of Pentecost. As Pinnock puts it, "The isolated disciples were incorporated into the Spirit-filled Body of Christ."[14] Thus they became the agents of God's kingdom on earth. Otherwise, they would have been a bunch of Jesus disciples who perpetuated his teaching like any religious movement. The uniqueness of the church is that it is empowered by the Holy Spirit. Nicholas M. Healy puts it this way: "What renders the church unique and superior to all other religious and non-religious bodies is what I have already noted in the passing, namely its Spirit-empowered *orientation* to Jesus Christ and through him, to the triune God."[15]

The presence of the Holy Spirit in the church implies that the mission of the church is the continuation of the mission of Christ. There could be no church without the power of the Holy Spirit, who is also called the spirit of Christ or Jesus (Acts 16:17; Rom 8:9; 1 Pet 1:11; Phil 1:19). This implies that a meaningful engagement with the world we live in is possible through the power of the Holy Spirit that empowered Jesus Christ if its mandate and model is the mission of Jesus Christ. The church

---

14   Clark H. Pinnock, "Church in the Power of the Holy Spirit: The Promise of Pentecostal Ecclesiology," *Journal of Pentecostal Theology* 14, no. 2 (April 2006): 150.

15   Nicholas M. Healy, *Church, World and the Christian Life: Practical-Prophetic Ecclesiology* (Cambridge: Cambridge University Press, 2000), 17.

should be considered not merely an association of people but the sphere where the Holy Spirit operates. The church cannot be imagined without the Spirit; a church without the Holy Spirit is no better than any other human organization.

This link between Christ and Holy Spirit is not a surprise to Indian Christian theologians. Christology and pneumatology are inseparably interlinked in traditional Indian Christian theology. As Kirsteen Kim highlights, Indian Christian theologians preferred the Spirit-Christology over the logos-Christology that was popular in the West. The former views Christ as not only the giver of the Holy Spirit but also the receiver of the Holy Spirit.[16]

Thus the presence of the Holy Spirit in the mission of Jesus and in the being and mission of the early church implies that ecclesiology should incorporate both Christology and pneumatology in order to have a proper understanding of the mission of the church. These three disciplines (Christology, pneumatology, and ecclesiology) should be treated in an integrated fashion. Isaac Zokoue suggests they should not be treated even as "three juxtaposed and disjointed disciplines" but inseparably dependent on one another.[17]

Though the experience of the Holy Spirit is an individual matter, it is evident in the New Testament that even the spiritual experience of the individual believer has a corporate dimension, and it is maintained by the community. The Holy Spirit came upon all of them while they were gathered and waiting for him in the Upper Room. Luke highlights the corporate dimension of the individual experience: "Divided tongues as of fire appeared to them and rested *on each one of them*. And *they were all filled* with the Holy Spirit and began to speak in other tongues as the Spirit gave them utterance" (Acts 2:3–4; emphasis mine). In other words, without the community, there is no experience of the Holy Spirit. The Holy Spirit constitutes the church, equips it by giving gifts, and directs its mission. Commenting on the theology of Yves Congar, Stephen Ebo Annan affirms not only that the church is constituted by the Holy Spirit but also that it has "a prominent role not only in the Church's bene esse

---

16  Kirsteen Kim, "Indian Contribution to Contemporary Mission Pneumatology," *Transformation* 23, no. 1 (2006): 31.

17  Isaac Zokoue, "The Church as Pneumatic Community: Toward an Ecclesiology for the African Context," in Chung and Noelliste, *Diverse and Creative Voices*, 158.

but also its very esse."[18] Annan also comments that the Holy Spirit continues its constitutive work, as it is not limited to one event. It is "a continuous recalling of the Spirit upon the Church."[19]

The church should realize that its power to transform everything according to God's plan comes from the Holy Spirit. There can be no theology of liberation that ignores a theology of the Holy Spirit, the liberator. A new vision of pneumatology is important for a theology of social transformation for various reasons other than its christological significance. The Holy Spirit breathes life into the church to send it to mission.

## The Holy Spirit and the World

How does the church carry out its mission in our world by the power of the Holy Spirit? First, it needs to realize that the Holy Spirit and sociopolitical structures are related. The Holy Spirit is present in all avenues of human existence. We cannot ignore this aspect of the Holy Spirit that operates through the structures of this world. As Simon Chan says, we should not just recognize this fact but also "cooperate with the Spirit in advancing the Kingdom of God in these structures."[20]

Second, the work of the Holy Spirit has a social dimension beyond the individual dimension. The popular tendency is to associate the Holy Spirit with its role in salvation, holy living, sanctification, and so on. Though this aspect of the work of the Holy Spirit cannot be overlooked, the role of the Holy Spirit who gives gifts to individuals to empower them to do works of service should not be ignored either (1 Cor 12). So it is important to recognize that the corporate experience of the Holy Spirit is as important as the individual experience of the Holy Spirit. Many times, the individual, spiritual experience of the Holy Spirit gets priority over the corporate aspect of the Holy Spirit.

In a similar vein, it is important to realize that the Holy Spirit is given for the benefit of the body of Christ and for those outside the church. After studying the various gifts of the Holy Spirit in 1 Corinthians 12, Jeffrey T. Snell concludes that the ministry of the Holy Spirit is

18  Stephen Ebo Annan, "'Do Not Stifle the Spirit': The Vision of Yves Congar for Charismatic Ecclesiology," *New Blackfriars* 95, no. 1058 (2014): 453.

19  Annan, 453.

20  Simon Chan, "Mother Church: Toward a Pentecostal Ecclesiology," *Pneuma* 22, no. 2 (September 2000): 206.

not limited to the body of Christ. He summarizes that the activity of the Holy Spirit "is not limited only to the sphere of the individual believer or even the Church but extends to the whole creation."[21] So it is important to discern the work of the Holy Spirit to transform lives outside the body of Christ, in the wider world of human existence.

Though we realize that the Holy Spirit is at work in the structures outside the church, we should also realize that it is not a spirit of the natural realm. Behind every social, political, or economic structure, there is something that animates it. It could be ideologies, persuasions, and so on. We should concede that the Holy Spirit is different from all these spirits that govern this world. Elaborating on the fact that on the day of Pentecost the Holy Spirit "came from heaven" (Acts 2:2), Zokoue stresses this essential character of the Holy Spirit. He observes that "the Holy Spirit does not emerge from the bosom of humanity; he is not of earthly origin, and he cannot, therefore, be comparable to the spirits which haunt this world."[22]

## Empowering Community

The church continues the mission of Christ in the power of the Holy Spirit as a community of not only empowered people but also empowering people. The church is a place where the powerless are empowered to perform their God-given tasks in the world. The early church is an example of what God can do with a bunch of powerless, ordinary people when they are constituted as a community. The power of the individual ensues from the power of the community. Using military imagery, Dutch theologian Abraham Kuyper imagined church as the table from which the soldiers eat and drink to refresh when tired of the battle outside the church: "The church is rather like the army tent of the Lord where soldiers strengthen themselves before that battle, where they treat their wounds after the battle, and where one who has become 'prisoner by the sword of the Word' is fed at the table of the Lord."[23] The church thus exists to empower individuals for their God-given engagement with the world.

---

21  Jeffrey T. Snell, "Beyond the Individual and into the World: A Call to Participation in the Larger Purposes of the Spirit on the Basis of Pentecostal Theology," *Pneuma* 14, no. 1 (1992): 48.

22  Zokoue, "Church as Pneumatic Community," 151.

23  Abraham Kuyper, *Rooted & Grounded: The Church as Organism and Institution* (Grand Rapids, MI: Christian's Library Press, 2013), loc. 602 of 888, Kindle.

## The Missional Church

If the church is a community of believers that continues the mission of Jesus Christ, empowered by the same Holy Spirit that empowered him, it should be a missional church. The adjective *missional* entered theological discussion through the works of Darrell L. Guder.[24] Christopher J. H. Wright suggests that "missional is to the word *mission* what covenantal is to *covenant*, or fictional to *fiction*."[25] Current theological discussions have expanded to new fields by attaching this adjective to nouns like *theology*, *hermeneutic*, and so on. Our focus here is on the "missional church." When used as an adjective of the church, it signifies mission as the very essence of the church or its being.

A church where mission is only one of the branches or programs is not a missional church. Guder clarifies that "to describe the church as 'missional' is to make a basic theological claim, to articulate a widely held but also widely ignored consensus regarding the fundamental purpose of the Christian church. Rather than seeing mission as, at best, one of the necessary prongs of the church's calling, and at worst as a misguided adventure, it must be seen as the fundamental, the essential, the centering understanding of the church's purpose and action."[26]

A missional church's self-understanding is shaped by its notion of the *missio Dei*. Guder opines that the conception of *missio Dei* means that the mission of the church is developed after the pattern of the mission of God, "who calls and empowers his people to be the sign, foretaste, and instrument of God's new order under the lordship Christ."[27] In this conception, the church is the witness of Christ, sent by him to the world for which he gave his life.

This missional imagination is important for the church to be an agent of integral transformation. First, the group of believers "gathered in his name" should understand that they are a missional community—mission is their raison d'être. Second, they should also believe that the mission for which they are constituted by the Holy Spirit is the integral transformation

---

24  Darrell L. Guder, ed., *Missional Church: A Vision for the Sending of the Church in North America* (Grand Rapids, MI: Eerdmans, 1998).

25  Christopher J. H. Wright, *The Mission of God: Unlocking the Bible's Grand Narrative* (Downers Grove, IL: IVP Academic, 2006), 24.

26  Darrell L. Guder, *Called to Witness: Doing Missional Theology* (Grand Rapids, MI: Eerdmans, 2015), 67.

27  Guder, 73.

of the society in which they are situated. Only this self-image will help the community of believers make any transformative impact.

## Church in the Model of Trinity

The *missio Dei* leads us from the mission of God to the nature of God. It seems that there is almost a consensus, certainly among Trinitarian theologians, that the Godhead reflects the church in the world. Not only that, but as Johannes P. Deetlefs states, "The 20th century has witnessed a revival of interest in the doctrine of the Trinity and its significance for human life."[28]

The missional nature of the Trinity is evident in the action of each person of the Godhead. For example, the Father sent the Son into the world (John 3:16). The Son returned to the Father (John 16:10) so that the Father and the Son can send the Holy Spirit into the world (John 14:26; Acts 2:33). At the same time, they are one. The unity of the Triune God is clear in the baptism as well as the prayers of Jesus (Matt 3:13–17; Mark 1:9–11; Luke 3:21–23; John 17:22).

The missional church should be imagined in a Trinitarian model for various other reasons as well. First, in contrast to polytheistic or other monotheistic faiths, the Bible understands the Godhead as the Trinity, which is essentially social and thus relational. God is one but also a unity of three persons in a mutual relationship. The Trinity is also conceived as a relationship of mutual love, as the community of believers is called to be (John 17:24–26). This nature of the church is what prepares it for engagement in the world.

The missional church continues the mission of the Triune God, and its mission is rooted in the nature of the Triune God. Niemandt expresses a near consensus that "mission does not belong to the church, it is not something people do—it is a characteristic of the Triune God."[29]

However, there are various ways Trinitarian theologians see the relationship within the Trinity. Some models conceive of the Trinity in a hierarchical structure, where one person precedes others, and in the other, the

---

28  Johannes P. Deetlefs, "Political Implications of the Trinity: Two Approaches," *Hervormde Teologiese Studies* 75, no. 1 (2019): 1.

29  Cornelius J. P. Niemandt, "Trends in Missional Ecclesiology," *HTS Teologiese Studies* 68, no. 1 (2012): 3.

social Trinitarian model, all persons are equal. All these models do reflect the structure and relationships of the church.

A theology of integral transformation is interested in explaining not church structures but how the church should engage in the mission of God in the world of its existence. The model that Volf proposes, which is widely discussed, is more interested in this aspect of the Trinity. Volf's model is developed in conversation with the models proposed by Joseph Ratzinger and John Zizioulas. After examining these two dominant models of the Trinity, Volf concludes that "the structure of trinitarian relations is characterized neither by a pyramidal dominance of the one (so Ratzinger) nor by a hierarchical bipolarity between the one and the many (so Zizioulas), but rather by a polycentric and symmetrical reciprocity of the many."[30] In the polycentric model, we see equality, mutuality, and love.

Volf's ecclesiology, developed according to this model of the Trinity, has many merits. As we have seen, the church needs the power of the same Spirit that empowered Christ. As Jaroslav Z. Skira has commented, Volf's model leads to an ecclesiology that "favors the pneumatological."[31] This ecclesiology also aims to give women their due place in the church. Volf declares, "A major strand of my argument stands in close affinity with this egalitarian agenda of feminist ecclesiology."[32] His model of ecclesiology also addresses the major threat that individualism poses to the church globally. Though he is critical of the Trinitarian models of Ratzinger and Zizioulas, he agrees with their critique of individualism. The concept of the Trinity strikes a proper balance between individualism and community. In the Trinity, the three persons do not lose their individuality, but they are a community together through perichoresis, or interpenetration. In our world of increasing individualism, which has penetrated the church, the Trinitarian conception of the Godhead is of immense relevance. He thus suggests that the Trinitarian model must be appreciated in the wider context of these issues of contemporary importance.

Volf's model of Trinity and its corresponding ecclesiology has found wide acceptance among those who advocate the church's engagement with society. This model is opposed to totalitarianism. As Paul S. Fiddes

---

30  Volf, *After Our Likeness*, 217.
31  Jaroslav Z. Skira, "After Our Likeness: The Church as the Image of the Trinity," *Theological Studies* 60, no. 2 (June 1999): 376–77.
32  Volf, *After Our Likeness*, 2.

comments, "The Christian idea of the Trinity has the potential for challenging and undermining this domination of the One. It forbids us from conceiving of God as the absolute individual, the solitary Father, the supreme Judge who provides support to a powerful human individual in his image."[33]

As Rian Venter points out, this presents the Trinity as inclusive and hospitable and embraces diversity and generosity.[34] Volf and those who follow him endorse the Eastern Orthodox conception of the relationship within the Trinity, which is one of perichoresis. This concept denotes that the three persons interpenetrate or permeate one another without confusion or without losing their individuality. David S. Cunningham points out that Volf's model of the Trinity leads to "an egalitarian ecclesiology that will, nevertheless, remain critical of contemporary individualism."[35]

The Trinitarian relationship of love among the three persons is the model for a just society. One of the unique features of the Trinity is its mutuality. Though the Trinity is a community of three distinct persons, none can be defined without reference to the other. They affirm one another and even surrender to one another. We see here individuality, love, and mutual submission. The Trinity thus models an ideal society.

Volf reminds us that the church in the Trinitarian model is a church that serves one another. He says, "The symmetrical reciprocity of the relations of the trinitarian persons finds its correspondence in the image of the church in which all members serve one another with their specific gifts of the Spirit in imitation of the Lord and through the power of the Father. Like the divine persons, they all stand in a relation of mutual giving and receiving."[36]

## The Place of Hierarchy

If the church is focused on the mission of God and its relationships reflect the polycentric, social Trinity, then what is the place of offices and the

---

33  Paul S. Fiddes, *Participating in God: A Pastoral Doctrine of the Trinity* (Louisville, KY: Westminster John Knox, 2000), 66.

34  Rian Venter, "Speaking God Today: The Adventures of a Rediscovered Trinitarian Grammar," Inaugural lecture, University of the Free State (UFS), Bloemfontein, South Africa, April 2011, 15–16.

35  David S. Cunningham, "After Our Likeness: The Church as the Image of the Trinity," *Theology Today; Princeton* 57, no. 1 (April 2000): 123.

36  Volf, *After Our Likeness*, 219.

members who constitute the transforming church? What does such a community of believers look like? The first thing that comes under scrutiny is the role and place of hierarchy in a missional church. It is evident by now that a polycentric, Trinitarian conception does not accommodate hierarchy in the church in any form.

Moreover, hierarchy is paternalistic, as it does everything for the people without allowing the people to do anything for themselves or one another. It stands in the way of believers becoming a community in which there is equality and mutual sharing as in the early church. Some historians of Christianity hold that Nicea and the subsequent reimagining of the church as an appendage of Constantine's empire made hierarchy a necessary evil of the church. As a consequence, the church left its call to serve the world in order to serve the political interests of the empire. Historians of the Christian church have always acknowledged that the conversion of Roman emperor Constantine and the church becoming the official state religion turned the church into an appendage of the state that served the state's interests. Alexandre J. M. E. Christoyannopoulos portrays the impact of this on Christian mission in rather sarcastic terms: "Christ, who had turned the Roman empire upside down, was turned into a lap-dog for the Roman emperor."[37] Hierarchy is thus the church aping the political structure of the empire to serve the interests of the empire rather covertly. Annan cites Congar, saying that the church "is not a pyramid whose passive base receives everything from the apex."[38]

The Trinitarian vision of equality, mutuality, and love negates any hierarchy. A vision of the Trinity where all persons of the Godhead are equal negates the dominance of any one person in the Godhead and so in the church. The model of the Trinity that we endorse is not the only reason for imagining the church without hierarchy; there are various other reasons a hierarchical model of the church is not conducive to integral transformation. Hierarchy robs the people of their power as it creates dependency on itself. However, though they appear to be all powerful, hierarchies also have limits. As the case study on the eradication of caste discrimination shows, the main reason the initiatives of the hierarchy failed is that they could not push the laity beyond a certain level. The laity

---

37  Alexandre J. M. E. Christoyannopoulos, *Christian Anarchism: A Political Commentary on the Gospel*, abridged ed. (Exeter, UK: Imprint Academic, 2011), 70.

38  Annan, "Do Not Stifle the Spirit," 456.

protested and the whole endeavor collapsed, proving that the real power rests with the people, not the leaders.

The church, with all its hierarchies and bureaucracies, is not conducive to acting as an agent of transformation. As Elliott comments, "The church acts as an enormous clobbering machine." It discourages activists who, according to him, "suffer at the hands of hierarchies and bureaucracies which, exhibiting little of the freedom and the joy Christ entrusted to his apostles, secure the status quo and along with it, their own survival."[39]

As already noted, Volf's model doesn't endorse individualism as a substitute for hierarchy, which may thrive in the absence of the latter. Andy Lord says that Volf's ecclesiology "reacts against individualism and hierarchical holism."[40]

Participatory churches rather than hierarchical ones are the need of the time. The diminishing role of the hierarchy is the feature of ecclesiology that the churches are gravitating toward in the non-Western world. This "ecclesiological shift," as Volf calls it, makes new churches move away from the hierarchical models and toward "participative models of church configuration."[41] The church that is emerging in the Global South is the movement of the subalterns. As I try to illustrate in the epilogue, in India the church is growing among the underprivileged and the social outcasts in the urban slums and the poor in rural areas. So it is important to give the subalterns their due place in what the church is to be and to ensure their voices are heard.

The two case studies on sati and caste in the history of the Indian churches prove that hierarchy is ineffective in social transformation. At the same time, these case studies illustrate that empowered and enlightened ordinary members can transform society even before the juggernaut of the church hierarchy begins to roll. When it did roll, it only widened the cracks along the fault lines.

---

39  Elliott, *Freedom, Justice*, 210.
40  Andy Lord, *Network Church: A Pentecostal Ecclesiology Shaped by Mission* (Leiden: Brill Academic, 2012), 69, citing Volf, *After Our Likeness*, 3.
41  Volf, *After Our Likeness*, 12.

## Autonomy of the Local Community

Imagining the church without the weight of the hierarchy leads us to two other important aspects of being a church. One is the autonomy of the local community, and the other is the autonomy of the individual.

Autonomy means freedom from coercion from a dominant system or individuals. In addition to freedom from coercion, it also implies the ability to make independent decisions sensitive to the context. Social scientists seem to agree that despite globalization, local issues still dominate human life. The autonomy of the believing community paves the way to make faith contextual. Such communities are the seedbeds of genuine contextual theologies.

The autonomy of the local community is not just a matter of its governance but also directs its inner life. Clarke suggests that worship and liturgy must be democratized by liberating them from ritual specialists and releasing them to the people. This is an important aspect of the autonomy of the local community. He says, "Proper worship in the Indian context is not a law that needs to be discerned by the specialist and made binding on the people."[42] Clarke seems to be in agreement with Volf, who argues, "The presence of Christ does not enter the church through the 'narrow portals' of ordained office, but rather through the dynamic life of the entire church."[43]

## Autonomy of the Individual

The autonomy of the local community should not mean that it is replacing the hierarchy and imposing its own powers on the individual. The church structure and confessions must empower persons of average ability to engage in God's work of liberation.

The autonomy of the individual means freedom from cohesion even within an autonomous community. Autonomy allows the individual the freedom to speak and share the power with the rest of the members of the community. The autonomy of the individual within the autonomous community is not new but has precedence in the early church. Paul claims that he did not consult anyone when he launched his mission after the risen Christ met him on the Damascus Road. He says, "I did not

---

42  Clarke, "Hindutva," 221.
43  Volf, *After Our Likeness*, 152.

immediately consult with anyone; nor did I go up to Jerusalem to those who were apostles before me, but I went away into Arabia, and returned again to Damascus" (Gal 1:16–17). It took another three years before he met any of the apostles. His mission was an autonomous decision guided by the Holy Spirit. Similarly, when Paul and Barnabas parted ways—one into Jewish mission and another into mission to the gentiles—these were also individual decisions without the cohesion or consent of a higher centralized authority. However, history bears witness that both were part of God's plan for God's mission in the world.

The autonomy of the individual is important for social transformation. Autonomy is freedom; the opposite is slavery. Structures are controlled by those who oppress, and the collaborators of oppressors naturally mutes the voice of the oppressed. The oppressed can speak only if everyone is autonomous and exercises their right to speak.

Recovering the autonomy of the individual, which structures stifle, is the most important step toward integral transformation. The individual gets the vision and inspiration for social action from the community of faith. But only individuals with higher levels of autonomy can engage in social transformation. The community forms the individual with a transformative vision. Hierarchical church structures may stifle the autonomy of the individual. The liberating power of autonomy has been witnessed in history. We have already seen that subalterns in particular and Dalits specifically have been asserting their rights without a patronizing system. This is evident in movements of Dalit power, Dalit activism, and so on.

The autonomy of the community and the autonomy of the individual are interlinked. It is essential that only individuals with autonomy should form the community. The community of people empowered to think, act, and inspire on their own create the transformative community. Such communities inspire individuals and other communities to transform themselves and their contexts.

The autonomy of the individual and the autonomy of the community are the direct work of the Holy Spirit. It is the Holy Spirit, not the structures, that empowers individuals for liberation. It is the empowered followers of Christ that animate the structure, not vice versa. On the day of Pentecost, the empowering tongues of fire rested "on each one of them" (Acts 2:3), not just on the leaders of the movement. However, this individual empowerment leads to the formation of the community. When the Holy Spirit empowered the individuals, the community took birth: "All who believed were together and had all things in common" (Acts 2:44).

The autonomy of the individual doesn't mean individualism. Individualism is as dangerous as hierarchical structures. The church is a local assembly; the church exists only by being gathered together. Thus the church is against both individualism and hierarchical constructs. Volf further expounds on this: "Christ's presence through the Spirit makes a person into a Christian and simultaneously leads that person into ecclesial communion, constituting the church thus in a twofold fashion: first by adding a person to the church and, second, by mediating faith to others through that person. Here again we see that the church as mother and the church as sibling fellowship are identical."[44]

## Conclusion

In summary, we may see that in the reenvisioning of the church, the church is essentially a community where physical structures are not essential. The gathered community of believers continues the *missio Dei* of transformation empowered by the Holy Spirit that empowered Christ in this earthly mission. This community is autonomous but is also ecumenical, as it recognizes "one Lord, one faith, one baptism, one God and Father of all, who is over all and through all and in all" (Eph 4:5–6). Each member of this community is empowered by the Holy Spirit and empowered by the autonomous community that the Spirit has constituted. This community also empowers and releases its members to engage in integral transformation solely guided by the Holy Spirit.

---

44  Volf, 175.

# 7

# TAKING FAITH
# TO THE WORLD

We do not want a church that will move with the world. We want
a church that will move the world.

—G. K. Chesterton

## Transforming the Church in Its World

It is essential that the missional and autonomous community committed
to the transformation of society should also have a vision of the world
into which it is sent. First, any agenda for transformation is possible
only when we see the distinction between the world and the church.
The church should conceive of itself as something the world is not. This
distinction is the foundation of the church's mission to the world. Otherwise, the church becomes an association of people without any particular
raison d'être.

In a similar vein, in their functions also, the church and the world are
different. The church is what the world cannot be. It is undeniable that
the world is trying to evolve into a better place—morally, economically,
socially, and so on. In the Indian context, so much has been achieved by
the political and economic vision of its leaders since independence. But
all these are limited by human reason and the human capacity to imagine.
God's plan for a just society is beyond human reason and imagination, so
the church should lead the way by being God's agent of transformation
of life and its systems.

However, the church is called to lead the world, to show the way. At no point should the world and the church coalesce into one. The church has to be distinct in its mission because the world goes by what it sees, but the church, being the work of Christ, goes by faith. Besides this, there is certainly a qualitative difference between what the world can offer and what God can offer, as Jesus said about the peace that he gave: "Peace I leave with you; my peace I give to you. *Not as the world* gives do I give to you" (John 14:27; emphasis mine).

The church doesn't blend in with the rest of the society around it because the systems of this world need not always be just. Even when the world is close to being just, it need not sustain the just systems. This unpredictability demands that the church be alert always. As Lopez reminds us, the church is "an alternate society" that "emerges as a community of active resistance to the predominant religious and political system."[1] Furthermore, Healey suggests that for the church to maintain its prophetic voice, it should not fit into the "norms of non-Christian worldview or social context."[2] The kingdom of God should be evident in the church, where all differences of race, sex, age, and status that characterize the society around it must vanish.

Though the church is what the world is not and what the world could not be, it is important to listen to the world as well. We have already seen that the Holy Spirit is present in the world and its systems. Healy says, "Since the church can at times learn from the work of the Spirit working in what is non-church, it seems reasonable to propose that the church should make a habit of listening to the non-church, of trying to discern the Spirit's action in its challenges, of seeking out its wisdom in case Christ's word is spoken there."[3]

The Indian church should also be aware that there are other agents of liberation that God is using in our world. This is especially evident in India, where God used various agencies like the constitutional provisions and the religious and nonreligious reform movements for the upliftment of the subalterns. The church should be humble enough to listen to secular voices at work and even learn from them. Healy further adds that "the non-church world is thus not only the place where the church is to witness to its Lord, but is also the place from which the church may learn

---

1 Lopez, "Church as Liberated," 169.
2 Healy, *Church, World and the Christian Life*, 50.
3 Healy, 69.

about its Lord and about true discipleship."[4] As we have already discovered, the non-Christian world has a lot to say regarding the upliftment of the subalterns in India. The church must listen as it seeks its way forward in God's mission of transformation.

Another dimension of the church-world relationship is that the church should be willing to participate with all those who are interested in social transformation. These collaborators include non-Christian agencies. The abolition of sati, the campaigns against widow marriage, and so on are not exclusive battles of the church, though the lead role that the Christian faith had is undeniable. The church played an important role by bringing awareness and challenging the conscience of the reformers. But these battles against social evils were successfully fought by enlisting non-Christian reformers, the Fourth Estate, lawmakers, and so on. The church must view reformers of other persuasions as partners in mission rather than opponents or competitors. The lives of reformers like Phule and many others illustrate that Christian witness influenced them.

All of these observations convince us that the exploration of a theology of integral transformation cannot limit itself to Christian themes or limit itself to the church but must engage the world in which it lives and serves. It should address public issues that impact the lives of the oppressed. This conviction lands us in the realm of public theology. As Sebastian Kim and Katie Day argue, "If theology is only addressed to the church, and in language understandable only within the halls of academies, it does not touch lived life, and ceases to be relevant."[5]

## The Place of Public Theology

Martin E. Marty introduced the term *public theology* in 1974 to Christian theology circles while analyzing the works of Reinhold Niebuhr, who had written extensively on American public life and issues.[6] Though the coining of the term is unanimously credited to Marty, many scholars agree that the Christian church had been engaged in public theology long before that. For example, Kim observes that "throughout Christian

---

4  Healy, 69.

5  Sebastian Kim and Katie Day, introduction to *A Companion to Public Theology* (Leiden: E. J. Brill, 2017), 10.

6  Martin E. Marty, "Reinhold Niebuhr: Public Theology and the American Experience," *Journal of Religion* 54, no. 4 (1974): 332–59.

history, churches have engaged with the wider society and political institutions both as minority communities and as dominant bodies."[7] Many scholars agree that Saint Augustine's work *The City of God* is an early example of public theology. Others opine that the church fathers who responded to the Greek philosophies of their time were addressing their "public," the dominant philosophers then. The same can be said of the reformers who addressed the issues of the Roman Catholic Church that was their public. Undoubtedly, Christian theologies that are poised to be contextual must be public theology in some ways, since they explore how God interacts with the conditions of humanity to challenge it to transform according to God's will in its own specific contexts.

### Public Theology Defined

Though there is an emerging consensus on the importance of public theology, there seems to be no consensus on how this should be defined, as Dirkie Smit observes. He says that "there exists no single and authoritative meaning of public theology and no single normative way of doing public theology."[8] This uncertainty and multiplicity of definitions have to do partly with the contextual nature of public theology—no two contexts can be the same in all details. This lack of consensus also has to do with its essential flexibility, as its aims and methodologies are dictated by the time and space where it is made. Theology must be always contemporary and relevant to the immediate situations in which it is rooted. However, in general, public theology, as Williams puts it, has to do with the public relevance of Christian beliefs and doctrines.[9]

The main task of theology is to inquire how God interacts with human affairs and history. This constant interaction with the human context gives it the potential to transform our lives, systems, and structures. Instead of clarifying Christian doctrines, theology should show the relevance of these to public policy and governance that have a bearing on human life. Max L. Stackhouse argues that theology by its very nature is engaged with public issues. He suggests that "it is an argument regarding the way things

---

7  Sebastian Kim, "Public Theology in the History of Christianity," in Kim and Day, *Companion to Public Theology*, 40.

8  Dirkie Smit, "Notions of the Public and Doing Theology," *International Journal of Public Theology* 1, no. 3 (September 1, 2007): 443.

9  Williams, "Prophetic Public Theology," 159.

are and ought to be, one decisive for public discourse and necessary to the guidance of individual souls, societies, and, indeed, the community of nations."[10] In a similar vein, Kim defines public theology as "critical, reflective and reasoned engagement of theology in society to bring the kingdom of God for the sake of the poor and the marginalised."[11] Kim thus moves on to suggest that public theology is not a neutral reflection of public affairs. It should have a stated goal of transforming societies in line with the vision of the Christian gospel. Kim's vision of public theology is more specific.

Though public theology could be defined in terms of what it achieves, it can also be defined in terms of who does it. For example, Andries van Aarde argues that public theology is not limited to the professional (Christian) theologian, but the public also should join the enterprise, and it should adopt various formats. In another sense, it is public because it is done by the public in public![12] There will be evident differences between public theology done by the lay theologian and public theology done by the professional theologian. This difference is inevitable whichever way we understand the nature and goal of theology.

Public theology also assumes that theology should reach the public, who may not share the same language as theological academics. It should aim to reach beyond the academies to the common people. As Linell E. Cady suggests, theology must "move past the technical jargon that rendered it all but incomprehensible to those outside one professional guild."[13] This possibility of shifting the realm of theology to the public, in the style and language of the public, empowers the subalterns to articulate their concerns without any sophisticated academic qualifications. All that they need to know is that they should not compromise with their adversities but act as God's agents of transformation. In this way, public theology as an enterprise empowers the subalterns to find their voice.

---

10  Max L. Stackhouse, "Public Theology and Ethical Judgment," *Theology Today* 54, no. 2 (1997): 165.

11  Kim, "Public Theology," 40.

12  Andries van Aarde, "What Is 'Theology' in 'Public Theology' and What Is 'Public' about 'Public Theology'?," *HTS Theological Studies* 64, no. 3 (September 2008): 1215.

13  Linell E. Cady, "Public Theology and the Postsecular Turn," *International Journal of Public Theology* 8, no. 3 (August 26, 2014): 295.

Another important question is why we need theology to make an impact on public life when there are many other disciplines—like social sciences—that can do the same job, sometimes quicker and better. As Stackhouse argues, the logic of philosophical thought is vulnerable and can be distorted, so we need a public theology. Moreover, the logic of philosophical thought, social analysis, and moral judgment is unstable too, since it may not be grounded in God. He affirms that "the human wisdom of philosophy, the ordering systems of societies, and the ethical judgments of individuals may express the irrational elements of human fantasy no less than does private religion; and all of them need to be seen as subject to standards, purposes, and an unconditioned reality greater than our wisdoms, systems, judgments, and religions can generate or discover alone. 'Logos' requires 'theos.' Theology is required."[14]

A range of disciplines are committed to the upliftment of the Dalits and other subalterns in India. However, Christian public theology should also claim its due place among them instead of shunning or replacing them.

## Public Theology and Other Theologies

Public theology is not any theology that we make accessible to the public. The goal of public theology can be further clarified by delineating it from other theologies in Christian practice.

First, public theology is not dogmatic theology, which clarifies issues of faith and practice. Dogmatic theology addresses those who already possess the faith it tries to clarify. As van Aarde comments, "When the content of academic theology is filled with 'doctrinal truths,' the dialogue with public theology disintegrates on account of the asymmetrical discourse from which secularization wanted to depart. Therefore, public theology is not ecclesial theology. They do, however, overlap to some extent."[15]

Similarly, public theology should not be confused with polemic theology or apologetic theology, though they address the public. Public theology should distance itself from polemic theology, which attempts to pull down false understandings of faith. Its audience is those who do not believe or even oppose faith. In the same way, public theology should not be confused

---

14  Stackhouse, "Public Theology," 170.
15  Van Aarde, "What Is 'Theology'?," 1226.

with apologetic theology, which tries to clarify faith to those who are in doubt and necessarily oppose the faith. It tries to establish the reasonableness of faith and not public issues that impinge on human existence.

It is important that we refrain from narrowing down public theology to enhance the interests of the organized ecclesiastical institution. The goal of public theology is not "church planting" as such but is much wider. But at the same time, it is not aimed at merely bettering the lives of the marginalized and oppressed. Political ideologies, social movements, and so on are doing that job. It is aimed at a spirituality of transformation irrespective of organized religious institutions. It should be done in such a way as to improve the conditions of all those who are marginalized, disregarding religious benefits.

As we have seen, there should be a community that engages in and sustains transformation, but that should not be reduced to mere structures. The primary goal of public theology is not establishing such structures but effecting sustainable transformation. This makes one wonder if missional theology and public theology could be at loggerheads with each other. For some, missional theology advances the interests of the institution called church. In most cases, as George R. Hunsberger has observed, "mission does not seem likely to generate a robust engagement with the powers, with the critical issues that challenge a twenty-first-century democracy like ours."[16]

However, broadening the definition and goals of missional theology means that they could converge as well. Since public theology has to do with God's mission to the world, it has similar concerns to missional theology. Hunsberger goes on to explain that if public theology understands itself as "engaged in fulfilling the mission on which the church has been sent" and missional theology conceives of itself as "a sent community . . . placed squarely in the public life of the world," there can be no apparent conflict in the goals and interests of these theological approaches.[17] This understanding that the primary goal of mission is transformation makes public theology central to the missional church.

To effect the transformation of all areas of public life, public theology should be multidisciplinary—especially in India. Though it is a

---

16 George R. Hunsberger, "Can Public Theology and Missional Theology Talk to Each Other? Imagination and Nuance for the Church's Public Practices," *Cultural Encounters* 8, no. 2 (2012): 8.

17 Hunsberger, 7.

theology, the goal of public theology is not limited to taking "God talk" to the world. In an emerging society like India, public theology is an informed engagement with society, which requires engaging with all branches of human knowledge—science, philosophy, ethics, and so on. Felix Wilfred affirms this further: "In the context of multireligious and multicultural societies with fast transformation in the field of culture, economy, politics, etc., theology needs to interrogate itself regarding its responsibilities to the larger world. Traditional theology tends to cut everything—the world, society and culture—to its size, reminding us of the Procrustean bed!"[18]

Along these lines, Smit suggests that "studying the historical, the systematic and the legal issues involved, therefore, can be regarded rightly as important forms of doing public theology."[19] An overview of the issues of the *International Journal of Public Theology* ever since its beginning confirms that a wide variety of topics and themes have been the subjects of public theology.[20]

To be genuinely public, public theology should not only be multidisciplinary but express itself in all available formats, as van Aarde proposes. Public theology takes various forms: movies, songs, poems, novels, art, architecture, protest marches, clothing, and newspaper and magazine articles.[21] Envisioning public theology in multiple formats allows people from all walks of life, irrespective of their disciplines, to add momentum to the movement to effect an integral transformation of Indian society. These multiple formats would facilitate not only those who are literate but those in dominantly oral societies, particularly in India, to participate in and benefit from public theology.

## Doing Public Theology in India

We should narrow down the discussion of the nature of public theology in general to the specific situation in India. Public theology has an essential space in modern life, as religion continues to play a significant role, particularly in India. Gnana Patrick observes that even in the West,

---

18  Felix Wilfred, "On the Future of Asian Theology: Public Theologizing," in *Theology to Go Public*, ed. Felix Wilfred (Delhi: ISPCK, 2013), 35.

19  Smit, "Notions of the Public," 440.

20  *International Journal of Public Theology* is published by Brill Academic Publishers. ISSN: 15697320, 18725171.

21  Van Aarde, "What Is 'Theology'?," 1216.

"those who held on to anti-religious secular thought that religion would fade away as the secular modern thought progressed, have changed their positions."[22] However, in the case of countries like India, where religion always has been an inseparable part of life and society, it continues to play an integral role in the way people think and lead their lives. India has never seen a separation of state and religion but sees only increased interest in religion and its spread to more areas of human life than before.

Though public theology is a relatively new discipline, some consensus is emerging regarding the role of theology in public affairs in India. Felix Wilfred, a strong advocate for public theology in India particularly and Asia in general, argues that theology should have public relevance: "When theology does not bear upon public life, it is a failed theology. Such a theology is not only irrelevant, but could be most dangerous. Views maintained at the theological level have serious social and political consequences."[23] There are texts, structures, and policies beyond the control of the Christian church that impinge on the existential realities of the people. Indian Christian theology cannot overlook its responsibility to address these from a perspective of faith in God. Another Indian theologian, Pichalakattu Binoy, puts it succinctly: "It is a requirement for theology to go public."[24]

India has a tradition of public theological reasoning. Though M. M. Thomas never used the phrase *public theology*, his theology is the best example of one intersecting the boundaries of society and politics in India. Kim considers Thomas one of the pioneers of public theology in India.[25] A recent comprehensive study of Thomas's life and theological contributions published on his hundredth birthday provides insights into his theology on how faith and society ought to interact.[26]

---

22  Patrick Gnana, *Public Theology: Indian Concerns, Perspectives, and Themes* (Minneapolis: Fortress, 2020), 16.

23  Wilfred, "Future of Asian Theology," 52.

24  Pichalakattu Binoy, "Christianity, Civil Society and Science-Theology Dialogue in India," in *Indian Christianity and Its Public Role: Socio-theological Explorations*, ed. Gnana Patrick (Chennai, India: Department of Christian Studies, University of Madras, 2019), 211.

25  See Kim, "Public Theology."

26  Jesudas M. Athyal, George Zachariah, and Monica Melanchthon, *The Life, Legacy and Theology of M. M. Thomas: "Only Participants Earn the Right to Be Prophets"* (London: Routledge, 2016).

Though they had no access to the phrase *public theology*, elements of public theology can be traced in the works of many Indian theologians, such as P. D. Devanandan, Paulos Mar Gregorios, and others. A thorough study of the contribution of Indian theologians to public issues and life should be a separate project in the context of the rising interest in public theology in India.[27] Some would even add American Methodist missionary to India E. Stanley Jones to the list of Indian public theologians of the past.[28]

A Christian public theology, particularly in India, must be free from the trappings of political power; it should not be on the side of any political party or political persuasion. Politics in general, especially in India, is interested in the next election. So it is rightly called "electoral politics," and its goal is short term. Since the goal of public theology is to effect long-term, radical transformation, it should not get entombed by narrow political interests.

Public theologians should realize that the political power of the state is not the absolute authority, but the moral governance of God is. In actual politics—the brand of politics that we witness in our everyday lives in India—one party makes moral and political judgments on the others and tries to convince the electorate that their claims are more desirable. Public theology should disengage from such entanglements and should give priority to the moral judgment of God. Vernard Eller suggests that "our political action would be submission to God's moral judgment upon everything and everyone human."[29] It is important for public theologians to maintain this neutrality while at the same time prioritizing the kingdom values that the gospel upholds.

P. T. Mathew is very optimistic that "the pluralistic and democratic society which we have in India seems to offer a fertile ground to explore

---

27  Some of the works worth exploring in this regard are Paul Verghese, *The Secular Ideology: An Impotent Remedy for India's Communal Problem* (New Delhi: ISPCK, 1998); Madathilparampil Mamen Thomas, *The Secular Ideologies of India and the Secular Meaning of Christ*, Confessing the Faith in India Series (Madras, India: Christian Literature Society, 1976); and P. D. Devanandan and M. M. Thomas, *Christian Participation in Nation Building* (Bangalore, India: CISRS, 1960).

28  Stephen A. Graham, *The Totalitarian Kingdom of God: The Political Philosophy of E. Stanley Jones* (Lanham, MD: University Press of America, 1998).

29  Vernard Eller, *Christian Anarchy: Jesus' Primacy over the Powers* (Grand Rapids, MI: Eerdmans, 1987), xiii.

the possibilities of public theology."[30] The issues of oppression, exploitation, inequality, and injustice are all in the realm of Indian politics, religion, and nationalism. So any theology that deals with the pain of the suffering masses should address these domains of human existence, and that is exactly what public theology is poised to do.

One of the major problems with public theology in India has to do with its language and audience, as K. C. Abraham points out: "Although our theologians write on public issues, their writings seldom reach an audience outside the boundary of the churches. It has a public character, but 'consumers' are largely church people—at best students in the theological colleges."[31] This demands that theology done for the suffering masses in India must be at their level and in their language.

We need a public theology, since the issues that cause social inequalities belong to wider Indian society and culture and are not limited to Christians or the Christian church. They have originated outside Christian spirituality and thought and should be addressed in the wider arena of public life. Public theology should speak to the powers, especially the state, that inadvertently perpetuate the caste system.

India offers a unique space for public theology aimed at integral transformation. These are in the areas of the federal nature of the Indian republic, the unique nature of its secularism, and the context of religious pluralism. All these aspects of Indian democracy are interlinked as well. Next, we will take a closer look at these aspects of Indian society in envisioning the role and impact of public theology in India.

### Indian Federalism

India is a union of thirty-six entities—twenty-eight states and eight union territories. Federalism is a way of sharing power between the central government on one side and the states and union territories on the other. According to the Constitution of India, the legislative powers are divided into three lists—the Union List, the State List, and the Concurrent List. The Union List has ninety-eight items on which the Indian Parliament has the exclusive power to legislate. At present, the State List has

---

30  P. T. Mathew, "Indian Christianity and Its Public Role," in Patrick, *Indian Christianity and Its Public Role*, 92.

31  K. C. Abraham, "Asian Public Theology: Its Social Location," in Wilfred, *Theology to Go Public*, 17.

fifty-nine items that come under the power of the states. The Concurrent List has fifty-two items that have to be considered by both the union and state governments. These lists give Indian democracy a healthy balance of powers. The union or the central government cannot overrule the constitutional powers of the states, except in the event of the president's rule in the state. The union makes sure that each state is governed in accordance with the provisions of articles 355 and 256 of the constitution. At the same time, the states cannot violate the laws of the union and the constitution, which may lead to imposing the president's rule in the state, where the president of India takes over the administration of the state.

In a centralized federation, the constitution has vested so much power in the center.[32] The center has the power to form the states, decide their borders, create new states from existing states, and so on. It can also control the affairs of the state through the appointment of governors and the All-India Services—the bureaucracy appointed by the federal government. However, so much independence and power are still vested in the states and union territories.

However, the power vested in the center by the constitution has been indirectly regulated by the political parties. Tarun Gogoi notes that "India as a federal polity with parliamentary political system, political parties are playing a very crucial role as a significant intervening variable to influence the nature and working of India's federal process."[33] Another aspect that checks the center from drifting toward a unitary nation is the emergence of regional parties and coalitions. Gogoi observes that during 1989–2019, regional parties played a greater role in forming government at the center.[34] This happened as the two major coalition fronts, United Progressive Alliance (UPA) and National Democratic Alliance (NDA), included several regional parties, resulting in power sharing. The regional parties had to be given cabinet positions depending on the number of seats they won at the election. This has strengthened their voice for regional concerns at the national level, resulting in the states gathering more power in the federal arrangement. Though the center still holds constitutional power over the states, the interest of states cannot be disregarded in policy matters.

---

32 Tarun Gogoi, "Indian Federalism with Party System: Changes and Continuity," *International Journal of Scientific and Technology Research* 9, no. 1 (2020): 180.

33 Gogoi, 185.

34 Gogoi, 184.

A good example of the independence of the states in policy decisions is the response of the states to the Citizenship Amendment Act (CAA). The government of India enacted the CAA on December 12, 2019. According to this act, the Hindu, Sikh, Jain, Parsi, Buddhist, and Christian migrants from Afghanistan, Bangladesh, and Pakistan who entered India before 2014 are eligible for citizenship. By specifying some religious communities, it excludes Muslims and other communities, like Tamil refugees from Sri Lanka, Rohingyas from Myanmar, and Tibetan refugees. Protesters consider this act unconstitutional and a violation of human rights.

Though the protests against this and also against the National Register of Citizens are at a popular level, many states moved resolutions against the act.[35] Some states also challenged the act in the Supreme Court of India.[36] As of 2021, seven states in India have passed resolutions against this act of the central government, beginning with the state of Kerala. Though foreign policy and consequently citizenship is in the Central List, the states exercised their freedom to protest as federalism implies.

It seems that federalism, regardless of how we classify and interpret it, functionally is in good health in India. However, rising Hindu nationalism is indeed a growing threat to it. At least some people think that the threat is looming large, casting doubt as to whether the unitary forces shouting the "one nation" slogan will overtake it soon.

Though India is a religiously plural nation, this plurality is uneven as well. In reality, the religious minority on a national level is a religious majority in some states and a significant minority in other states. For example, Christians, which make up only approximately 3 percent of the population, are a minority at a national level. But they are the majority in most of the northeastern states; in Nagaland, 98 percent identify themselves as Christian. In Meghalaya, another northeastern state, 75 percent of the state's population are Christians. Even in states like Andhra Pradesh, Telengana, and Tamil Nadu, where Christians are in a minority, they are very visible in the politics and social life of the state. The same is the case

35  Press Trust of India, "Kerala Assembly Passes Anti-CAA Resolution in Assembly," India Today, accessed January 20, 2021, https://www.indiatoday.in/india/story/kerala-cm-tables-anti-caa-resolution-in-assembly-1632845-2019-12-31.

36  Al Jazeera, "Kerala State Challenges India's Citizenship Law in Supreme Court," accessed January 20, 2021, https://www.aljazeera.com/news/2020/1/14/kerala-state-challenges-indias-citizenship-law-in-supreme-court.

in Kerala, where they are in third place following Hindus and Muslims with 18 percent of the population, yet they have a strong presence in the political and cultural life of the state. Though Christians are a national minority in India, they have a very insignificant role in public affairs, particularly in areas where they are a majority or a significant minority. They need not be a majority on a state level, but there are pockets of Christian influence even in Christian minority states.

India is plural not only religiously but also racially and socioeconomically. Dalits and tribals dominate some states, and some regions are more economically backward than others. This reality of uneven plurality in all imaginable aspects of human life offers great scope for Christian public theology. Coupled with the federal nature of the Indian Republic, it creates oases where the Christian faith can make its public appeal and make its voice heard nationally. This reality of asymmetrical pluralism, coupled with the space that federalism offers, is a check on the march of majoritarianism on the national scene. This emboldens people to work for their own welfare in their own way independent of a unitary regime.

The federal nature of Indian democracy facilitates public theology and also impacts the Indian conscience. Federalism offers an immense opportunity for integral transformation. At the same time, Indian federalism is under threat from pseudonationalistic forces, and public theology has the responsibility to buttress federalism.

## Religious Pluralism

As federalism secures plurality in the union of India, the aspect of religious plurality demands a closer look. Will theology that emerges from a Christian minority be heard over the clamor that the religion of the majority makes at a national level, particularly when Hindu nationalism is on the rise? However, being a minority in a religiously pluralistic world should not be considered intimidating; rather, Indian Christians should see it as a great opportunity.

Religious pluralism demands due recognition of other faith traditions in the task of transformation. In a world where every religion makes truth claims to prove their moral superiority over others, the Bible doesn't deny that other religions have moral values. That is the basic principle that underlies the concept of general revelation. Paul affirms in the Epistle to the Romans that God has made himself known in the human conscience, creation, and culture (Rom 1:18–21). This, however, doesn't negate that human cultures and religions need direction and enrichment of these moral values. But Christians also should acknowledge that some of these moral values that God has deposited in other religions can be enriched and channeled for the public good.

However, most religions limit themselves to the realm of the metaphysical and tend to ignore matters of this world. Public theology must be in dialogue with other religious traditions to make them address public life. Rowena Robinson agrees that "one must look for, reflect on and relate to other religious theologies in a dialogue that is not merely framed as 'Christianity in an inter-religious context' but as Christian theology in an inter-theological conversation."[37]

In addition, we should also have a positive attitude toward other religions when they are open to others. Michael Amaladoss suggests that all religions—including the Christian faith—should make room for others, at least theoretically. This leads to the possibility of dialogue and collaboration in the public space. This collaboration among religious traditions need not be restricted to the religious sphere but can take place in the secular sphere as well. The concept of the unity of God that all religious traditions hold offers the framework for dialogue and collaboration in the public space.[38] Thus followers of other religious traditions could be collaborators in Christian public theological enterprises.

The idea of religious convictions interfacing with issues of public life is not new in India. Mahatma Gandhi's political decisions were undoubtedly motivated by his religious convictions, including the message of Jesus Christ. M. M. Thomas, whom we may consider a pioneer of public theology in India, saw the presence of Christ not only in other religions but also in secular movements.

There are various ways in which Christian faith can help religions engage in doing public theology for the good of the public. Christians should help religions free themselves, as Amaladoss suggests, from the "pressures of negative secularists and religious fundamentalists." We also must recognize that religions are the sources of "values and of inspiration

---

37  Rowena Robinson, "Asian Public Theology: Its Social Location," in Wilfred, *Theology to Go Public*, 11.

38  Michael Amaladoss, "Public Theology in a Multi-religious Society," in Wilfred, *Theology to Go Public*, 86–87.

and empowerment in upholding them." We also need "to free religion from its historical and socio-cultural conditionings."[39]

Such a goal of partnering with the dominant religious structures in India will help Christian theologians raise the issue of caste and other practices that promulgate evils in society under the vestiges of religion. Public theology in the domain of religion will help them see that caste is not religious but has cultural conditioning. I will reserve a detailed examination of this for the following section.

Conscientizing the followers of other religions of their social responsibility is not paternalistic. It stems from a humble recognition that all religions have the potential to be socially responsible. One of the aims of Christian public theology is to help religious traditions use their resources to oppose and transform oppressive values and structures. We have already seen that in the bygone era, such approaches to challenging sati and other social evils in Indian society had a positive impact on Indian society.

However, we should also realize that the general revelation is only a step in the move toward the special revelation of Jesus Christ. So all societies should evolve toward the kingdom ideal that Jesus Christ preached. We should always remind ourselves that the ultimate goal of public theology, as Kim puts it, is "to bring the kingdom of God for the sake of the poor and the marginalised."[40]

Religious pluralism is not a threat or intimidating. It provides the space where public theologians can meet potential collaborators who acknowledge God in human affairs.

### Secularism

While religious pluralism presents the opportunity to partner with people of other religions for the integral transformation of society, the particular nature of secularism in India makes it even more feasible.

In many countries in the neighborhood, like China and Myanmar, religion is not allowed to have any place in public affairs. At the same time, in some other neighboring countries, religion controls politics and public life—evidently in Pakistan and to some extent in Sri Lanka. However, the case in India is different. India is a secular society, where secularism is defined as a respect for other religions rather than a clean divide

---

39 Amaladoss, 96.
40 Kim, "Public Theology," 40.

between the state and the church. It can be described, as D. John Romus calls it, "humanistic secularism."[41]

Humanistic secularism does not separate religion and state but has a healthy distance between the two. Moreover, there is room for the interaction of the state in the affairs of religions "to help or regulate them without the inclination to control or destroy them."[42] This leads the state to grant financial aid to educational institutions run by religious minorities. At the same time, the state does intervene in matters of religion when the religious policies stand in the way of human dignity and progress. For example, in the past, the state has intervened in religious practices like temple entry to all castes and genders. This also applies to enacting laws on widow marriage, banning child marriage, and so on. Though these had religious warrants for at least some segments, the state intervened to abolish them, disregarding narrow religious sentiments. In recent years, the Supreme Court of India has ordered that women should be allowed in Hindu temples, where they were not allowed for religious reasons.

So Indian secularism is more than freedom of religion and the state's nonintervention in religious matters. It is committed to religious diversity. As Rajeev Bhargava observes, it has "a commitment to multiple values, namely liberty, equality, and fraternity."[43] Moreover, it provides religious communities the right to establish educational institutions to maintain their religious traditions. These educational institutions with the distinct flavor of their respective religious communities not only serve their members but have a wider impact, as they are open to the public.

Public theology should thrive in the space that secularism offers in India, but it is not without responsibilities. Public theology should protect secularism from attempts to replace it with the dominance of one religion to the disadvantage of others. Many social thinkers argue that Indian secularism is under threat from various quarters. The main threat comes from emerging religious fundamentalism and religious nationalism. The antisecular sentiments of the Bharatiya Janata Party (BJP) and the Sangh Parivar are so real that they cannot be ignored. Sumit Ganguly

---

41  D. John Romus, "Public Theology: Perspectives from the Indian Constitution," in Wilfred, *Theology to Go Public*, 136.

42  Romus, 136.

43  Rajeev Bhargava, "Can Secularism Be Rehabilitated?," in *Secular States and Religious Diversity*, ed. Bruce J. Berman, Rajeev Bhargava, and Andre Laliberte (Vancouver: UBC Press, 2013), 82.

opines, "The BJP and its associated organizations have fostered a significant body of antisecular sentiment, and have exploited failures and omis-
sions by Congress in order to do so."[44]

The goal of public theology should also be to protect it from its
critics. Ganguly perceives that there is growing apathy among Indian
intellectuals who perceive secularism as foreign, which he argues should
be replaced by "an ethic of religious tolerance" drawn from India's own
traditions.[45] Secularism is not freedom to practice religious faith, nor is
it the neutrality of the state toward religions, considering them all to be
equal. Secularism is that aspect of the nation where religions are free to
play their role in society. It is more than tolerance of one another. Secularism provides a level ground for all religions to improve the lives of individuals and society. Secularism is so powerful that it makes antisecular or
pseudosecular forces budge.

Public theology must be concerned about the apathy in real life to
the principle of secularism that is enshrined in the constitution. Though
secularism is held highly as an ideal, some political observers think that
no political party is really committed to its principles. Before the 2014
election that brought the BJP to power, Anand Teltumbde commented
that "indeed, no party in India in the present milieu can really be called
secular."[46] That is true, because the image of India's secularism was a mere
slogan for political parties.

The discourses that weaken Indian secularism are on the rise. The
healthy balance in the relationship between religion and state is a great
opportunity for public theology in India. So the priorities of Christian
public theology are, first, to sustain the secular nature of the Indian
democracy and, second, to utilize the space and opportunities it provides
to allow Christian faith to have a bearing on social realities.

### Public Theology of Human Dignity

A wide spectrum of issues that affect public life could be the subjects of
public theology in India. These issues will multiply as human history

---

44  Sumit Ganguly, "The Crisis of Indian Secularism," *Journal of Democracy* 14,
    no. 4 (October 2003): 21.

45  Ganguly, 22.

46  Anand Teltumbde, "More Than Secularism," *Economic and Political Weekly* 49,
    no. 19 (2014): 11.

moves forward. The varying contexts and changing social and political realities will keep public theology busy. However, there is one issue that has remained persistent over the millennia in Indian history that affects everyone and every aspect of human existence across the religious landscape. That is the issue of caste, which has become an inseparable component of the Indian psyche. It is not only practiced in Hinduism, but converts in all religions still carry caste with them and are treated according to their caste status in their host religions. This is an issue of human dignity and equality that is marred by religion. This is paramount, since all other issues of injustice, oppression, and exploitation stem from this larger issue. Though caste is invented and imposed by the privileged sections of society, it is the Dalits who particularly have fallen victim to it. A. M. Abraham Ayrookuzhiel points out that the Dalits are guided by "a mythological consciousness promoted by the Brahmanical religion."[47]

As noted earlier, though Dalit theology has tried to address caste-based discrimination, it has left the structure of caste and the mindset behind it untouched. On the contrary, we also have seen the laudable theological contributions made by European missionaries and Dalit converts to Christianity in challenging the caste system in the period before Dalit theology was born.

Human equality and dignity are not new issues for theology, nor are they specific to India. But these issues have a particular nature in India because dignity and equality in society are something that persons fall victim to by virtue of their birth. No one has any control over their birth into specific castes that culture has designated as low or high. Children born into rich Dalit families are considered of lower rank than the poor Brahmins in the neighborhood. High-ranking officers, political decision-makers, or influential thinkers from low-caste backgrounds still carry their caste stigma irrespective of their status and contributions. In India, human dignity and equality are judged not by what a person can achieve but by the caste one is born into. This is the evil of the caste system.

It is wrong to think that caste consciousness affects only the lower castes. Caste has ramifications not only for the lower castes but for the entire society. The caste-based system of education, jobs, and so on has consequences for the upper castes as well. The preferential treatment that

---

47  A. M. Abraham Ayrookuzhiel, "Dalits Move towards the Ideology of 'Nationality,'" in *A Reader in Dalit Theology* (Madras, India: Gurukul Lutheran Theological College, 1990), 170.

the lower castes are granted in education, government, and jobs has a negative impact on the other castes, especially the higher castes. We have already seen that rising unemployment among the high castes, partly due to the reservation policy that favors the low castes, has made high castes take up jobs considered to be menial in Indian society, such as sanitation.[48]

Though Dalits are victims of caste, they are also villains at their expense. Paramjit S. Judge points out that the Dalits also are divided by their caste identities.[49] They are victims of a system that ascribes them less dignity than other humans, but the caste mindset that is so ingrained in the Indian psyche also makes the lower castes see other human beings with varying degrees of human worth and dignity. Caste is not just a vertical stratification as mandated by some Hindu scriptures but also horizontal. It is not just between upper and lower castes but also between castes and subcastes. Caste hierarchy has a mesmerizing effect. It makes people feel superior by comparing themselves with those who are below them. Moreover, each caste glories in its own caste identity irrespective of whether they are low or high in comparison to others. Intercaste rivalry is a daily occurrence. Intercaste marriages are the main reason for the honor deaths frequently happening in rural India.

Caste consciousness within the Dalit community is the reason for their self-defeat. Teltumbde has shown that caste consciousness within Dalit communities weakens the impact of their struggles. He observes that "hankering on caste identities serves ruling class interests and hence, benefits its patrons but fails to benefit the larger masses, who are victims of the caste system. The conclusion is inescapable: Unless Dalits transcend castes and forge a class unity with other marginalised people, their struggle can never reach fruition."[50]

Though caste originated in Hinduism, caste-based thinking is so strong that no religion could liberate itself from its curse. Caste is practiced by non-Hindu religions in India as strongly as in Hindu society. Converts to Sikhism, Islam, and even Christianity from the lower castes were treated with disdain by their host religions. Caste is the problem not

48  Babu and Prasad, "Six Dalit Paradoxes," 25.
49  Paramjit S. Judge, "Hierarchical Differentiation among Dalits," *Economic and Political Weekly* 38, no. 28 (2003).
50  Anand Teltumbde, "Azadi Kooch: Towards a New Grammar of the Dalit Struggle," *Economic and Political Weekly* 52, no. 31 (August 5, 2017): 11.

just of wider society but also of Christian churches. The prevalence of caste in the churches is a visible reality; it is documented by participants from the Caste Affected Countries in Bangkok (2009) who confessed that their churches were also affected by caste. The declaration says, "The representatives of the churches of the countries more directly affected by caste wished to confess their complicity with CBD [Caste Based Discrimination] and to acknowledge that caste remains deeply entrenched in their churches today. This is manifested in leadership struggles, use of resources, unwillingness to challenge the authorities and failure to support victims of caste atrocities."[51]

Besides confessing the presence of casteism in the churches, the Bangkok Declaration called upon the Dalits to give up casteism practiced between subcastes. Part of the declaration that is addressed to the Dalits is as follows: "We call upon you to practice unity with steadfastness and courage, both inside and outside the churches, to avoid division by 'sub-caste' and leadership competition, and to present a broad-based and democratic front in the liberation struggle. We also call upon you to act in solidarity with other struggles for justice."[52]

Caste is a major threat to human equality and dignity in Indian society, since it destroys harmony, it divides, and it scorns human equality and dignity. Ironically, it prevails in Christian churches as in other religious groups. It is time for the Christian faith to confront this mindset.

There are various theories about the origin of caste in India.[53] Though the goal of theology is not to debate the origin of evil but to eliminate it, some historical perspective will help in developing a public theology against this social evil. The caste system could have existed as early as the fifteenth century BCE. The earliest textual evidence of the caste system in India is dated to the *Purusha Sukta* of the *Rig Veda*. Though the exact date of this Sukta is debated, a conservative date would place it between 1400 and 1000 BCE. Originally, the caste system was a system of division of labor. But it has become, as Lourdunathan comments, "a division of the

---

51 "The Bangkok Declaration and Call: Statement from the Global Ecumenical Conference on Justice for Dalits, March 21–24, 2009, Bangkok, Thailand," World Council of Churches, March 21, 2009, https://www.oikoumene.org/resources/documents/the-bangkok-declaration-and-call.

52 "Bangkok Declaration and Call," 7.

53 See Ekta Singh, *Caste System in India: A Historical Perspective* (Delhi: Kalpaz, 2005). For a short overview on the various theories of caste, see Barman, "Caste Violence in India," 195.

labourers."[54] The *Rig Veda* only explains the origin of the fourfold division of society. It doesn't explain the origin and status of those outside this system, nor does it advocate any discrimination.

Scriptural warrants were provided for caste-based discrimination by the ninth to the seventh centuries BCE. By the time of the Upanishads, hatred of Dalits rose to a new level. These texts, dating from the sixth or seventh centuries BCE, describe Dalits as dogs and as those born in dirty wombs.[55] At the same time, the higher castes were said to be born in pleasant wombs. The Upanishads thus promoted hatred against the Dalits. *Manusmriti*, dated between 1 and 700 CE, promoted this segregation and hatred further. J. H. Anand suggests that *Manusmriti* is almost equal in status to the Apostles' Creed to Christians, as it is so fundamental to Hindu belief and conduct, where disobedience is sin.[56]

The reports of Chinese travelers attest that caste discrimination was deeply rooted in Indian society by the middle of the Common Era. Fa-Hien, who visited India between 405 CE and 411 CE, reports that the despised castes (Chandalas) were segregated from others and had to live in separate quarters. Yuan Chwang, the Chinese traveler who visited India in 629 CE, also confirms the segregation.

The religious nature of caste in its origin, perpetuation, and practice should be the concern of public theology as it reaches out to the Hindu conscience and all those who follow it as part of their culture. Christian public theology should challenge the non-Christian worldview by upholding the biblical vision of the equality and dignity of human beings. It should motivate followers of other religions to critically reexamine and deconstruct their religious resources in this regard.

It is far from the truth to assume that all religious scriptures of India vouch for caste-based discrimination. A wealth of religious resources, besides the Smritis, Upanishads, and Vedas, uphold a caste-free view of the world and also give people of low castes due significance. Public

---

54  Lourdunathan, *Hermeneutics*, 157.

55  The dates of the Hindu religious texts are highly contested. The dates mentioned here represent the majority view and are broad rather than specific. This applies particularly to the dates of the Upanishads and *Manusmriti*.

56  J. H. Anand, "Law Versus Grace—Theological Aspects of Dalit Poetry," in *Doing Theology with the Poetic Traditions of India: Focus on Dalit and Tribal Poems*, ed. Joseph Patmury (Bangalore: PTCA/SATHRI, 1996), 100.

theologians must pay attention.[57] People of low birth have played important roles in Hindu epics and are duly venerated irrespective of their caste identity. For example, Vyasa, who authored *Mahabharata*, is of a lower caste. According to tradition, Satyavati, who is the mother of Vyasa, was of low-caste origin. She was born in the fishermen community. Her father (Dusharaj) was a fisherman. She also happens to be the great-grandmother of the Pandavas and the Kauravas, who are the main characters of *Mahabharata*. According to the Hindu notions of caste, cowherds are of lower caste. But Krishna, who happens to belong to the tribe of cowherds, is venerated as lord. Lord Krishna has a huge following in the Hindu religion, particularly among the Vaishnavites and the related sects and cults. It may seem an irony that his devotees consider themselves of higher caste by birth, ignoring the fact that the object of their devotion is of low caste—a good example of the mismatch between religious and social realities.

Though it is certain that a religious worldview is the reason for caste and caste-based discrimination, it received political validation during the colonial period. Nicholas B. Dirks argues that though caste had a long history, the present form of it comes from colonial times.[58] Dirks points out that the solidification of caste happened in the colonial period under the influence of writings of anthropologists and ethnographers.[59] Colonial historiographers, ethnographers, and so on have noted the phenomenon of caste hierarchy in India. The colonial writers were not critical of the evils of caste, but they took it as normative in Indian society.[60] Colonial bureaucrats turned caste, which was fluid earlier, into a political construction that served the purpose of categorization and delimitation. Caste was not made by the British, but caste as we know it is a British construction.

This means that in the colonial period, caste obtained new political significance. Caste politics and caste violence go back to this colonial heritage. The politics of caste that the colonial rulers invented became a convenient tool for the rulers of independent India, who rather unconsciously perpetuated caste and its attendant injustice and inequality.

---

57  See Vettam Mani, *Puranic Encyclopaedia: A Comprehensive Work with Special Reference to the Epic and Puranic Literature*, 10th ed. (Delhi: Motilal Banarsidass, 2015).

58  Nicholas B. Dirks, *Castes of Mind: Colonialism and the Making of Modern India* (Princeton, NJ: Princeton University Press, 2002), 18.

59  Dirks, *Castes of Mind*. See, particularly, the chapter "Ethnographic State."

60  Dirks, 13–15.

Indian politics failed to eradicate caste, but it tried to remove caste-based disabilities like untouchability and so on. As Babu and Prasad point out, "Despite the state's public stand against caste, what it had set forth as its task was the mere removal of caste-based disabilities, such as untouchability, and 'compensate' its victims within a narrowly defined framework."[61] However, in this process of alleviating the pain of caste, it indirectly strengthened caste identities in its attempt to compensate for caste-based inequalities. Babu and Prasad suggest that instead of eradicating caste, the Indian state wrote caste into law and thus gave it permanence.[62] Now even the parties that claim to be secular use caste as a convenient tool in electoral politics. Politics in India is caste politics.

All this means that the fight for human equality and dignity is not only to be fought in the arena of religion. It is also a political issue that public theology should deal with by transforming political reasoning in India. Christian public theology should thus address caste-based politics, using the poor as vote banks, and so on. It is time now that Christian theologians join public discourse and rearticulate the biblical vision of the equality of all human beings, the equality of genders, and the equity and harmony of the human family. Only then can Christian witness have any public relevance and the church become God's agent of integral transformation.

## Conclusion

A theology aimed at effecting integral transformation in India should be a public theology. It should address public issues and challenge the oppressive power structure, whether religious, cultural, or political. The nature of Indian democracy—particularly federalism, secularism, and plurality—is very conducive to public theology. It gives Indian theologians the space that Mars Hill offered Paul to address the philosophers of Athens.

In particular, religious pluralism in India offers the Christian witness partners to work toward transforming all aspects of Indian society so that the kingdom of God may overtake all aspects of its being. Though the issues that any Christian public theology must address will be determined by time and context, the issue of caste is paramount, since it has persisted

---

61   Babu and Prasad, "Six Dalit Paradoxes." 24.
62   Babu and Prasad, 24.

over the millennia and is a major component of the Indian psyche. So one of the uncompromising aspects of Christian public theology in India would be that of human equality and dignity. It involves deconstructing religious myths perpetuating human inequality and also highlighting religious texts that transcend caste thinking besides constantly confronting the Indian politics of caste.

# CONCLUSION

We began by surveying the salient aspects of Dalit liberation theology. The founders envisaged it as a contextual countertheology with the goal of liberating the Dalits from their plight. It belongs to the tradition of other movements, like liberation theologies, Black theology, and Minjung theology. Dalit theology shows marks of influence from all of these. Dalit theology was not limited to those who had actual experience of Dalit pathos, but the enterprise was open to all who were interested in alleviating the pain of the Dalits. So this theological venture thrived with the participation of non-Dalits as well as persons from Dalit backgrounds who may not have had firsthand Dalit experience. It is still not clear if the enterprise addressed the issues of Dalits in the churches, or Dalits in society, or both.

In order to achieve its purpose of emancipation, it was crucial to give Dalits their voice in their own way. So it was essential to pose it as a theology counter to the theologies that were not concerned with contextual realities, especially the Dalit condition. So it was proposed that it should counter the existing dominant Indian theology, considered to be Brahmanical in its concerns and methodology. Though their hopes were high and they were eager to see a hermeneutical revolution in Indian theology, Dalit theologians did not venture beyond hermeneutical methods, akin to liberation theologies elsewhere in the West. Since they did not go beyond the familiar and available, in the long run, Dalit theology turned out to be reading the Bible from a Dalit perspective using sophisticated methods inaccessible to the ordinary person. By mostly limiting themselves to the interpretation of biblical texts, the Dalit theologians left untouched the other textual and nontextual structures that perpetuate discrimination.

Moreover, these Dalit readings left out many important themes that were inevitable for any theological endeavor aimed at the transformation of oppressive contexts. It lacked a holistic Christology in light of the entire Christian canon that stretches beyond Jesus's incarnation and crucifixion to his resurrection and dominion over the powers of darkness. It was heavily criticized for not confronting the church by failing to develop an adequate ecclesiology. The third person of the Trinity was sadly ignored as well.

The Dalit theology that emerged in the 1980s ignored theological reflections on Dalit issues by European missionaries and natives in the bygone era. Probably the enthusiasm to be a countertheology was the main reason for this blind spot. In its zeal to counter Christian theology couched in the Brahmanical traditions, it ignored the trails blazed by earlier non-Brahmanical theologians who addressed the issues of suffering, especially that of the Dalits. Instead of a continuity that would have been fruitful, it deprived itself of the great legacy of earlier theological reflections that shared its goals. It also failed to draw momentum from Dalit discourses in the secular academy and the Dalit movements for liberation happening all around it. Overlooking non-Christian ideologies and movements that were sailing in the same direction as Dalit liberation led it to stagnation.

A skewed view of Dalit reality is another reason Dalit theology could not log much mileage. Though there were creative proposals regarding its methodologies, Dalit theologians in general continued to use Dalit pathos as their master key for hermeneutical endeavors. In their passion for the Dalit pathos, Dalit theologians ignored other aspects of the Dalit reality. They overlooked the fact that historically, Dalits in particular and all subalterns in general are people of power who can assert themselves and have the potential to engage in struggles for liberation and transformation of society. They were not always passive victims. This myopia resulted in a failure to harness the power of the oppressed, attested to by their history of challenging their adversities. Dalit theology stagnated because it ignored the ever-changing social, economic, and political scenarios of India and the subcontinent. Dalits are emerging by their own power and by the various policies of the state that were committed to correcting the disadvantages of age-old neglect.

Dalit liberation theology in general limited its scope to the suffering of the Dalits, ignoring the larger issues of society. It also limited itself by not addressing those who have perpetuated the injustices the Dalits and wider society suffered. Moreover, though it educated the church about the suffering of the Dalits, it did not propose an ecclesiology that would equip the church to engage in God's mission for integral transformation.

The critical overview of Dalit theology's enterprise is not meant to disregard its historical significance. Dalit theology educated theologians and the Indian church about the plight of the subalterns in society and the church. Without the daring steps taken by the founding fathers of Dalit theology and the contributions Dalit theologians made over four decades, Indian Christian theology would have remained as God talk, irrelevant to ground realities. Dalit theology inaugurated a new trajectory of theological pursuit in India that seeks to alleviate human suffering and envision a better world.

Though Dalit theology made Christian academia take a strategically important turn toward addressing contextual realities, it hasn't made much headway. However, this should not be dispiriting. It may need new sails and oars to pull it out of its lull. The trajectory that Dalit theology has set out must be followed by incorporating themes that are important for an integral transformation of the conditions and structures of oppression. Its scope should be widened from liberation to integral transformation, which aims to liberate the oppressed while at the same time transforming all that is evil. It should look at the human condition much more broadly, transcending caste and social barriers. It should make new partners. The history of oppression and the struggles of the oppressed reviewed here should convince us that all who are oppressed have the power to liberate themselves and to be agents of transformation. Not patronization but partnership should be the goal of theology designed to achieve transformation.

Indian Christian theology aimed at the integral transformation of society needs to redraw its concerns and content. Only then can it surge toward new horizons with new enthusiasm, vigor, and hope. First, we need to reimagine the church in India in order to equip it for this new voyage. The church should be conceived of essentially as a group of people under the lordship of Christ, committed to continuing his mission in the world. The church's power to transform the world comes from the Holy Spirit, who empowered Christ and his disciples. Since it continues the *missio Dei*, it reflects the Trinity in its structure and relationship—one of equality and mutual love. Thus the missional, transforming church is essentially an autonomous community of Spirit-empowered individuals who carry on the mission of God in ways relevant to their contexts.

Second, the church as God's agent of integral transformation should also bring its faith to bear on human realities outside its walls. This requires that it make its voice heard in public to address public affairs that determine the quality of human existence. Public theology is not limited to the Christian academy but also partners with the non-Christian world to better human conditions. These include enhancing the shared positive moral values of all religious confessions and engaging in the hermeneutical task of interpreting religious texts and nontexts to eradicate social evils and improve human conditions. Two salient aspects of Indian democracy—namely, its federal nature and its secularism—provide public theology a fertile ground besides religious pluralism, which ensures the place of religion in public life in India. Though any issue that has public relevance could be the subject of public theology, the particular context of India demands that equality and human dignity should be the priorities of public theologians in India as they confront the issue of caste ingrained in the Indian psyche.

Things have to change. As John F. Kennedy said, "Change is the law of life and those who only look to the past or present are certain to miss the future."

# EPILOGUE—IT'S HAPPENING!

Envisioning integral transformation is not a pie in the sky; it is a ground reality. Spirit-empowered, autonomous individuals in autonomous communities of Christ disciples, transforming their world to be a better place, are attested all over India. Though this is happening without the direct involvement of Christian theological input, there is increasing academic interest in this new phenomenon among secular sociologists, anthropologists, and economists.

In this part, I would like to highlight two such case studies done by secular sociologists. The first case study is from northwestern India, and the second is diagonally across, from the far southeast. They are not just isolated cases, but they testify to what is happening all over India, from north to south and east to west. Both have to do with the Dalits and particularly the doubly disadvantaged Dalit women who have to suffer as Dalits and also as women.

## The Bhils of Rajasthan

Sabreswar Sahoo, a sociologist with the Indian Institute of Technology, Delhi, studied the conversion among the Bhil tribes in Rajasthan over many years.[1] The dominant Rajput Hindu community holds this tribal community in total disdain. Sahoo's book is based on extensive ethnographic fieldwork done among the Bhils, which included interacting with the converts and the leaders of the various mission movements. Though his main interest was in explaining the reasons for the antipathy of the

---

1 Sarbeswar Sahoo, *Pentecostalism and Politics of Conversion in India*, 1st ed. (Cambridge: Cambridge University Press, 2018).

Hindu nationalists leading to violence against Christians in South Rajasthan, he has portrayed the silent social revolution that is shaking the foundations of caste and injustices of all sorts.

Various native missionary movements, mostly led by evangelists from the southern states, whom Sahoo calls "Pentecostals," have been engaged in missionary activity among the Bhils of Rajasthan over the years. *Pentecostalism* is an umbrella term that Sahoo uses to designate Christianity that is independent of mainline churches. However, they share many features of the Pentecostal movement worldwide, like the work of the Holy Spirit in the lives of individuals and the community, the autonomy of the local believing community, an absence of hierarchical structures, and so on. In reality, none of the movements that Sahoo studied have been extensions of Western Christian movements, including Pentecostalism. None of them even have "Pentecostal" in the names of their organizations! For example, two major movements that have impacted the lives of the Bhils that Sahoo studied are the Native Missionary Movement, founded by Thomas Matthews, and the Calvary Covenant Fellowship Mission (CCFM), founded and led by Manohar Kala.

The conversion to Pentecostalism has changed the self-perception of this community. Sahoo writes, "Religious conversion and association with the church have provided tribal Christians with confidence and hope, and made them optimistic. They found their new-found identity empowering."[2] He further notes that the Christian principles these communities uphold have transformed people's lives and "have generated hope to bring material as well as spiritual prosperity in the lives of poor tribals."[3]

Though the Bhil tribe is patriarchal like the Hindu society around them, their new experience of Christ has altered their gender relationships; especially to the advantage of women. Sahoo observes that "as a consequence of such teachings, the relationship between husband and wife in Pentecostal households, compared to the tribal Hindu household, is more equal. Because of this 'gender-egalitarian impulse' of Pentecostalism, women enjoy more freedom and autonomy."[4]

These movements have empowered all, particularly women. Sahoo reports the question one of the leaders of these movements posed to him during the interview. The respondent retorted, "If our Prime Minister,

---

2 Sahoo, 47.
3 Sahoo, 48.
4 Sahoo, 110.

President and the leader of the Congress Party can be women, why cannot women lead the church?"[5] True to this conviction, women are empowered to take up roles in their Christian community, family, and society.

Sahoo sums up his findings as follows: "For the converts, the Pentecostal church has provided an egalitarian space for all, without discriminating against anyone. It is in the church that the converts feel equal in the eyes of the Lord; it is where they sit, pray and eat together as a community of believers. In a sense, Pentecostalism has helped adivasis to convert to 'modernities.'"[6]

## Dalit Women in the Slums of Chennai

While the previous case study is from the rural areas of the northwestern corner of India, the second story comes from the urban center in southeastern India: Chennai, the capital of Tamil Nadu. Karin Kapadia has studied the growth of Pentecostalism among the women in the Dalit slums in Chennai since 2010.[7] She is a social anthropologist associated with the Oxford School of Global and Area Studies, University of Oxford. During a period of nine years, she made two visits annually to study this revolution, which began in the 1970s. Though this article was published in 2019, it is part of an ongoing study.

The story begins in the slums in Chennai when Dalit men who were the sole breadwinners began to lose their traditional jobs as head load workers and porters as technology and consequently the economy slowly changed to their disadvantage. As men began to lose their jobs, Dalit women had to enter the job market and earn enough to support their families. Consequently, the lives of the Dalit women became very stressful. The jobless or underemployed men continued to exert their authority over the women and their households; most of them had turned into alcoholics who depended on their wives' meager income. The jobless men, who thought their dignity was under threat, began to harass the women.

At this juncture, some non-Dalit pastors from the new and independent Pentecostal churches came to their streets, ignoring the rules

---

5  Sahoo, 112.
6  Sahoo, 158.
7  Karin Kapadia, "'Mirrored in God': Gramsci, Religion and Dalit Women Subalterns in South India," *Religions; Basel* 10, no. 12 (December 2019).

of untouchability and caste inequalities. The prayer groups that they established attracted many Dalit women suffering psychologically and economically. These prayer groups evolved into support groups led by Dalit women for the Dalit women and men. Later, they turned into care cells and churches. Since these churches were dominated by Dalit women, outsiders called them "female churches." These groups empowered women to pray without the help of "ritual experts," read the Bible, and use the Bible to teach and encourage other Dalit women. Many Dalit women who were semiliterate or illiterate began to learn to read the Bible only to read it to others.[8]

These churches were financially independent and free of any hierarchies.[9] They changed the gender equation, as women played active roles in the churches as evangelists, counselors, and so on. Dalit women are given public roles as lay pastors, group leaders, and so on. This has given them growing confidence in themselves. Kapadia comments, "Dalit women's growing confidence in the public roles they have accessed as lay teachers, lay preachers, and lay leaders in the liberating spaces of their Dalit Pentecostal churches have slowly enabled them to challenge male power in the arena where it is strongest—the domestic sphere. This is where Indian democracy must begin, within the four walls of the home."[10]

Kapadia sees that the Pentecostal movement among the Dalits in Chennai is a political movement that is emancipatory. She observes, "It is precisely because the effects of Pentecostal conversion are clearly so liberating for Dalit women in terms of their own gender politics, and for both Dalit women and men, in terms of Chennai's race/caste politics, that I am arguing that we should see Dalit Pentecostalism as constituting not just a religious movement but also an emancipatory political movement."[11]

Kapadia also argues that this movement in the Chennai slums has nurtured female self-confidence. She calls the female churches "natural greenhouses for nurturing female self-confidence and a feminist sensibility."[12] These female churches, though they do not challenge male hegemony

---

8  Kapadia, 4.
9  Kapadia, 6.
10  Kapadia, 14.
11  Kapadia, 6.
12  Kapadia, 7.

directly, have created "an irresistible desire for emancipation from male control among ordinary, dispossessed Dalit women."[13]

Kapadia's study has also shown that they are challenging power equations imposed by caste as they invite Hindus from high castes to join them. As Kapadia points out, "The very fact that Dalit Pentecostal evangelists happily and proudly invite non-Dalit 'caste-Hindus' to join them in their new identity suggests how radically the relations of power have changed."[14]

Kapadia concludes that "Dalit Pentecostalism has enabled poor women to access a new mobility, both physical and intellectual, across the new public spaces and public roles created by the Pentecostal churches. This has given Dalit Pentecostal women greater physical freedom, a powerful sense of agency and, above all, an astonishing and radically new moral authority, allowing women to significantly change Dalit gender dynamics."[15]

These two representative case studies testify that ordinary people are shaking their shackles off as they meet Christ, the Light of the World. They are empowered by his Spirit and freed from the chains of organized church structures by liberating themselves on their own. They are liberative forces, and their societies are being transformed. Their communities, devoid of hierarchies, empower their members for action.

These communities challenge the power structures that enslave them and also emancipate the power structures themselves. The exponential growth of these communities is evidence of their missional thrust. These instances are not isolated but represent integral transformation happening all over India unaided and also not scrutinized by the Christian theological academia. The church in India just needs to join the mission of the Triune God in what the Holy Spirit is already doing among the poor and the exploited.

---

13  Kapadia, 14.
14  Kapadia, 15.
15  Kapadia, 15.

# Bibliography

Aarde, Andries van. "What Is 'Theology' in 'Public Theology' and What Is 'Public' about 'Public Theology'?" *HTS Theological Studies* 64, no. 3 (September 2008): 1213–1234.

Abraham, K. C. "Asian Public Theology: Its Social Location." In *Theology to Go Public*, edited by Felix Wilfred, 15–27. Delhi: ISPCK, 2013.

Ahmad, Imtiaz, and Shashi Bhushan Upadhyay. *Dalit Assertion in Society, Literature and History*. New Delhi: Orient Blackswan, 2010.

Aleaz, Bonita. "Expressions of Dalit Christian Identity." *Contemporary Voice of Dalit* 5, no. 1 (January 1, 2012): 25–44.

Al Jazeera. "Kerala State Challenges India's Citizenship Law in Supreme Court." Accessed January 20, 2021. https://www.aljazeera.com/news/2020/1/14/kerala-state-challenges-indias-citizenship-law-in-supreme-court.

Amaladoss, Michael. "Public Theology in a Multi-religious Society." In *Theology to Go Public*, edited by Felix Wilfred, 80–97. Delhi: ISPCK, 2013.

Anand, J. H. "Law versus Grace—Theological Aspects of Dalit Poetry." In *Doing Theology with the Poetic Traditions of India: Focus on Dalit and Tribal Poems*, edited by Joseph Patmury, 81–105. Bangalore: PTCA/SATHRI, 1996.

Anderson, Evangeline. "Turning Bodies Inside Out. Contours of Womanist Theology." In *Dalit Theology in the Twenty-First Century: Discordant Voices, Discerning Pathways*, edited by Sathianathan Clarke, Manchala Deenabandhu, and Philip Peacock, 199–214. New Delhi: Oxford University Press, 2010.

Anderson-Rajkumar, Evangeline. "Skin, Body and Blood: Explorations for Dalit Hermeneutics." *Religion and Society* 49, no. 2 (September 2004): 106–112.

Annan, Stephen Ebo. "'Do Not Stifle the Spirit': The Vision of Yves Congar for Charismatic Ecclesiology." *New Blackfriars* 95, no. 1058 (2014): 443–467.

Athyal, Jesudas M., George Zachariah, and Monica Melanchthon. *The Life, Legacy and Theology of M. M. Thomas: "Only Participants Earn the Right to Be Prophets."* London: Routledge, 2016.

Avari, Burjor. *India: The Ancient Past: A History of the Indian Subcontinent from c. 7000 BCE to CE 1200.* London: Routledge, 2016.

Ayrookuzhiel, A. M. Abraham. "Dalits Move towards the Ideology of 'Nationality.'" In *A Reader in Dalit Theology*, 169–180. Madras, India: Gurukul Lutheran Theological College, 1990.

Babu, D. Shyam, and Chandra Bhan Prasad. "Six Dalit Paradoxes." *Economic and Political Weekly* 44, no. 23 (2009): 22–25.

"The Bangkok Declaration and Call: Statement from the Global Ecumenical Conference on Justice for Dalits, March 21–24, 2009, Bangkok, Thailand." World Council of Churches, March 21, 2009. https://www.oikoumene.org/resources/documents/the-bangkok-declaration-and-call.

Barman, Rup K. "Caste Violence in India: Reflections on Violence against the Dalits of Contemporary India." *Voice of Dalit* 3, no. 2 (2010): 193–212.

Baron, Eugene, and Moses Maponya. "The Recovery of the Prophetic Voice of the Church: The Adoption of a 'Missional Church' Imagination." *Verbum et Ecclesia* 41, no. 1 (July 27, 2020): 1–9.

Bateman, Josiah. *The Life of the Right Rev. Daniel Wilson, D. D., Late Lord Bishop of Calcutta and Metropolitan of India.* London: J. Murray, 1861.

Batra, Shakti. *Bama: Karukku (a Critical Study).* Delhi: Surjeet, 2019.

Bhargava, Rajeev. "Can Secularism Be Rehabilitated?" In *Secular States and Religious Diversity*, edited by Bruce J. Berman, Rajeev Bhargava, and Andre Laliberte, 69–93. Vancouver: UBC Press, 2013.

Binoy, Pichalakattu. "Christianity, Civil Society and Science-Theology Dialogue in India." In *Indian Christianity and Its Public Role: Socio-theological Explorations*, edited by Gnana Patrick, 197–212. Chennai, India: Department of Christian Studies, University of Madras, 2019.

Bonino, Jose Miguez. "Latin America." In *An Introduction to Third World Theologies*, edited by John Parratt, 16–43. Cambridge: Cambridge University Press, 2004.

Brockington, J. L. *Hinduism and Christianity.* New York: Springer, 2016.

Bubash, Paul. "Dalit Theology and Spiritual Oppression: A Call to Holiness in a Universal Church." *Journal of Theta Alpha Kappa* 38, no. 2 (September 2014): 36–51.

Cady, Linell E. "Public Theology and the Postsecular Turn." *International Journal of Public Theology* 8, no. 3 (August 26, 2014): 292–312.

Carr, Dhyanchand. "Dalit Theology Is Biblical and It Makes the Gospel Relevant." In *A Reader in Dalit Theology*, edited by Arvind P. Nirmal, 71–83. Madras, India: Gurukul Lutheran Theological College, n.d.

Chakravarty, Praveen. "Rise of Hindutva Forces, Upper Caste Antagonism Catalyse Drive by Educated Dalits to Assert Their Identity." Firstpost. Accessed February 12, 2018. http://www.firstpost.com/india/rise-of-hindutva-forces-upper -caste-antagonism-catalyse-drive-by-educated-dalits-to-assert-their-identity -4335739.html.

Chan, Simon. "Mother Church: Toward a Pentecostal Ecclesiology." *Pneuma* 22, no. 2 (September 2000): 177–208.

Chandramohan, P. *Developmental Modernity in Kerala: Narayana Guru, S. N. D. P. Yogam, and Social Reform*. New Delhi: Tulika, 2016.

Christopher, K. W. "Between Two Worlds: The Predicament of Dalit Christians in Bama's Works." *Journal of Commonwealth Literature* 47, no. 1 (March 1, 2012): 7–25.

Christoyannopoulos, Alexandre J. M. E. *Christian Anarchism: A Political Commentary on the Gospel*. Abridged ed. Exeter, UK: Imprint Academic, 2011.

Clarke, Sathianathan. *Dalits and Christianity: Subaltern Religion and Liberation Theology in India*. New Delhi: Oxford University Press, 1998.

———. "Dalit Theology: An Introductory and Interpretive Theological Exposition." In *Dalit Theology in the Twenty-First Century: Discordant Voices, Discerning Pathways*, edited by Sathianathan Clarke, Manchala Deenabandhu, and Philip Peacock, 19–37. New Delhi: Oxford University Press, 2010.

———. "Hindutva, Religious and Ethnocultural Minorities, and Indian-Christian Theology." *Harvard Theological Review; Cambridge* 95, no. 2 (April 2002): 197–226.

———. "The Jesus of Nineteenth Century Indian Christian Theology: An Indian Inculturation with Continuing Problems and Prospects." *Studies in World Christianity* 5, no. 1 (1999): 32–46.

Cone, James H. *Black Theology and Black Power*. Maryknoll, NY: Orbis, 2018.

Conn, H. M. "Liberation Theology." In *New Dictionary of Theology*, ed. Sinclair B. Ferguson and David F. Wright, 387–391. Leicester, UK: IVP, 1988.

"Correspondence of John S. Hoyland (1887–1957), Quaker and Missionary, 1820–1958." Archives Hub. Accessed November 19, 2019. https:// archiveshub.jisc.ac.uk/data/gb159-ms733.

Cunningham, David S. "After Our Likeness: The Church as the Image of the Trinity." *Theology Today; Princeton* 57, no. 1 (April 2000): 122–125.

Damodaran, Harish. *India's New Capitalists: Caste, Business, and Industry in a Modern Nation-State.* New Delhi: Permanent Black, 2008.

Deetlefs, Johannes P. "Political Implications of the Trinity: Two Approaches." *Hervormde Teologiese Studies* 75, no. 1 (2019): 1–8.

DeSmet, Richard. "Fleeting Time and Sacrificially Produced Continuity in Vedic Brahmanism and in Early Christianity." *Indian Theological Studies* 19, no. 2 (1982): 119–144.

———. "Job's 'Insufferable Comforters' and the Law of Karma." *Vidyajothi Journal of Theological Reflection* 5 (1994): 308–318.

Devanandan, P. D., and M. M. Thomas. *Christian Participation in Nation Building.* Bangalore, India: CISRS, 1960.

Devasahayam, V. "The Nature of Dalit Theology as Counter Theology." In *Frontiers of Dalit Theology,* edited by V Devasahayam, 53–67. Delhi: ISPCK/Gurukul, 1997.

Dirks, Nicholas B. *Castes of Mind: Colonialism and the Making of Modern India.* Princeton, NJ: Princeton University Press, 2002.

Eller, Vernard. *Christian Anarchy: Jesus' Primacy over the Powers.* Grand Rapids, MI: Eerdmans, 1987.

Elliott, Michael C. *Freedom, Justice and Christian Counter-Culture.* Philadelphia: Trinity Press International, 1990.

Escobar, Samuel. *A Time for Mission: The Challenge for Global Christianity.* Carlisle, UK: Langham Global Library, 2013.

Fiddes, Paul S. *Participating in God: A Pastoral Doctrine of the Trinity.* Louisville, KY: Westminster John Knox, 2000.

Forster, Michael N., and Kristin Gjesdal. *The Cambridge Companion to Hermeneutics.* Cambridge: Cambridge University Press, 2019.

Gangaiah, K. "Emergence of Dalit Movements in Andhra and Dr. B. R. Ambedkar's Influence." *Proceedings of the Indian History Congress* 68, no. 1 (2007): 935–943.

Ganguly, Sumit. "The Crisis of Indian Secularism." *Journal of Democracy* 14, no. 4 (October 2003): 11–25.

Gogoi, Tarun. "Indian Federalism with Party System: Changes and Continuity." *International Journal of Scientific and Technology Research* 9, no. 1 (2020): 180–187.

Golijanin, Vedran. "Jesus Christ and the Minjung in Korean Liberation Theology." *Godišnjak, Journal of Faculty of Orthodox Theology* 2, no. 12 (2013): 51–72.

Graham, Stephen A. *The Totalitarian Kingdom of God: The Political Philosophy of E. Stanley Jones.* Lanham, MD: University Press of America, 1998.

Guder, Darrell L. *Called to Witness: Doing Missional Theology*. Grand Rapids, MI: Eerdmans, 2015.

———, ed. *Missional Church: A Vision for the Sending of the Church in North America*. Grand Rapids, MI: Eerdmans, 1998.

Healy, Nicholas M. *Church, World and the Christian Life: Practical-Prophetic Ecclesiology*. Cambridge: Cambridge University Press, 2000.

Hebden, Keith. *Dalit Theology and Christian Anarchism*. New Critical Thinking in Religion, Theology, and Biblical Studies. Farnham, UK: Ashgate, 2011.

Hogg, A. G. *The Christian Message to the Hindu—Being the Duff Missionary Lectures for 1945 on the Challenge of the Gospel in India*. London: SCM, 2010.

———. *Karma and Redemption: An Essay toward the Interpretation of Hinduism and the Re-statement of Christianity*. Madras, India: Christian Literature Society, 1970.

Hogg, William Richey. "Psalm 22 and Christian Mission: A Reflection." *International Review of Mission* 77, no. 306 (April 1988): 238–246.

Holeka, Matous. "Reading the Bible in Various Streams of Liberation Theology: Latin American Theology, South African Black Theology and Indian Dalit Theology." *Communio Viatorium* 56, no. 2 (2014): 169–196.

Hoole, Charles. "Bishop Wilson and the Origins of Dalit Liberation." *Transformation* 21, no. 1 (2004): 41–45.

Hoyland, John S. *A Book of Prayers: Written for Use in an Indian College*. London: Challenge Book and Picture Store, 1951.

———. *Indian Crisis; the Background*. Freeport, NY: Books for Libraries, 1970.

———. *Letters from India*. London: Swarthmore Press, 1919.

Hunsberger, George R. "Can Public Theology and Missional Theology Talk to Each Other? Imagination and Nuance for the Church's Public Practices." *Cultural Encounters* 8, no. 2 (2012): 5–18.

Ilaiah, Kancha. *Post-Hindu India: A Discourse on Dalit-Bahujann, Socio-spiritual and Scientific Revolution*. New Delhi: Sage, 2009.

Jaffrelot, Christophe. *India's Silent Revolution: The Rise of the Lower Castes in North Indian Politics*. Delhi: Permanent Black, 2003.

Jain, Meenakshi. *Sati: Evangelicals, Baptist Missionaries, and the Changing Colonial Discourse*. New Delhi: Aryan Books International, 2016.

Jeremiah, Anderson H. M. "Exploring New Facets of Dalit Christology: Critical Interaction with J. D. Crossan's Portrayal of Jesus." In *Dalit Theology in the Twenty-First Century: Discordant Voices, Discerning Pathways*, edited by Sathianathan Clarke, Manchala Deenabandhu, and Philip Peacock, 150–167. New Delhi: Oxford University Press, 2010.

Jesurathnam, Kondasingu. *Dalit Liberative Hermeneutics: Indian Christian Dalit Interpretation of Psalm 22.* New Delhi: ISPCK, 2010.

Judge, Paramjit S. "Between Exclusion and Exclusivity: Dalits in Contemporary India." *Polish Sociological Review* 2, no. 178 (2012): 265–279.

———. "Hierarchical Differentiation among Dalits." *Economic and Political Weekly* 38, no. 28 (2003). 2990–2991.

Kapadia, Karin. "'Mirrored in God': Gramsci, Religion and Dalit Women Subalterns in South India." *Religions; Basel* 10, no. 12 (December 2019): n.p.

Kapur, Devesh, Chandra Bhan Prasad, Lant Pritchett, and D. Shyam Babu. "Rethinking Inequality: Dalits in Uttar Pradesh in the Market Reform Era." *Economic and Political Weekly* 45, no. 35 (2010): 39–49.

Kim, Kirsteen. "Indian Contribution to Contemporary Mission Pneumatology." *Transformation* 23, no. 1 (2006): 30–36.

Kim, Sebastian. "Public Theology in the History of Christianity." In *A Companion to Public Theology*, edited by Sebastian Kim and Katie Day, 40–66. Leiden: E. J. Brill, 2017.

Kim, Sebastian, and Katie Day. Introduction to *A Companion to Public Theology*, edited by Sebastian Kim and Katie Day, 1–21. Leiden: E. J. Brill, 2017.

Kumar, M. Ashok. "Dalits Preaching to Dalits: Lutheran Modes of Combating Caste Marginality in Andhra, South India." *Indian Anthropologist* 45, no. 1 (2015): 61–73.

Kuyper, Abraham. *Rooted & Grounded: The Church as Organism and Institution.* Grand Rapids, MI: Christian's Library Press, 2013. Kindle.

Larbeer, Mohan P. "The Spirit of Truth and Dalit Liberation." *Ecumenical Review* 42, no. 34 (1990): 229–236.

Lobo, Lancy. *Religious Conversion and Social Mobility: A Case Study of the Vankars in Central Gujarat.* Surat, India: Centre for Social Studies, 1991.

Lopez, Dario. "The Church as Liberated and Liberating Community: A Primer for a Latin American Ecclesiology." In *Diverse and Creative Voices: Theological Essays from the Majority World*, edited by Sung Wook Chung and Dieumeme Noelliste, 160–178. Havertown, UK: James Clarke, 2015.

Lord, Andy. *Network Church: A Pentecostal Ecclesiology Shaped by Mission.* Leiden: Brill Academic, 2012.

Louis, Prakash. "Dalit Christians: Betrayed by State and Church." *Economic and Political Weekly* 42, no. 16 (2007): 1410–1414.

Lourdunathan, S. *Hermeneutics of Dalit Philosophy of Liberation*. Tamil Nadu, India: Vergal, 2015.

Lucas, Bernard. *Christ and Society*. London: Francis Griffiths, 1909.

———. *The Empire of Christ*. Charleston: BiblioBazaar, 2008.

———. *Our Task in India: Shall We Proselytise Hindus or Evangelise India?* Reprint, London: Macmillan, 1914.

Manchala, Dheenabandhu. "Expanding the Ambit: Dalit Theological Contribution to Ecumenical Social Thought." In *Dalit Theology in the Twenty-First Century*, edited by Sathianathan Clarke, Manchala Deenabandhu, and Philip Peacock, 38–54. New Delhi: Oxford University Press, 2010.

Marty, Martin E. "Reinhold Niebuhr: Public Theology and the American Experience." *Journal of Religion* 54, no. 4 (1974): 332–359.

Massey, James. "Ingredients for a Dalit Theology." In *A Reader in Dalit Theology*, edited by Arvind P. Nirmal, 145–150. Madras, India: Gurukul Lutheran Theological College, 1990.

———. *Towards Dalit Hermeneutics: Rereading the Text, the History and the Literature*. New Delhi: ISPCK, 1994.

Mathew, P. T. "Indian Christianity and Its Public Role." In *Indian Christianity and Its Public Role: Socio-theological Explorations*, edited by Gnana Patrick, 91–110. Chennai: Department of Christian Studies, University of Madras, 2019.

Mohan, P. Sanal. "Religion, Social Space and Identity: The Prathyaksha Raksha Daiva Sabha and the Making of Cultural Boundaries in Twentieth Century Kerala." *South Asia: Journal of South Asian Studies* 28, no. 1 (April 1, 2005): 35–63.

Murali, Kaviyoor. *Dalit Bhasha Nigandu (Dalit Language Lexicon)—Malayalam*. Kottayam, India: DC Books, 2010.

Muthaiah, P. "Politics of Dalit Identity." *Indian Journal of Political Science* 65, no. 3 (2004): 385–402.

Narayan, Badri. *Documenting Dissent: Contesting Fables, Contested Memories and Dalit Political Discourse*. Shimla: Indian Institute of Advanced Studies, 2001.

———. *Fascinating Hindutva: Saffron Politics and Dalit Mobilisation*. New Delhi: Sage, 2009.

———. "History Produces Politics: The 'Nara-Maveshi' Movement in Uttar Pradesh." *Economic and Political Weekly* 45, no. 40 (2010): 111–119.

———. "Imagining the Past and Reconstructing Histories." *Social Scientist* 35, nos. 9/10 (2007): 67–87.

———. *Multiple Marginalities: An Anthology of Identified Dalit Writings*. New Delhi: Manohar, 2004.

———. *Women Heroes and Dalit Assertion in North India: Culture, Identity and Politics*. New Delhi: Sage, 2006.

Nelavala, Prasuna Gnana. "Caste Branding, Bleeding Body, Building Dalit Womanhood. Touchability of Jesus." In *Dalit Theology in the Twenty-First Century: Discordant Voices, Discerning Pathways*, edited by Sathianathan Clarke, Manchala Deenabandhu, and Philip Peacock, 266–276. New Delhi: Oxford University Press, 2010.

Nelavala, Surekha. "Martin Luther's Concept of Sola Scriptura and Its Impact on the Masses: A Dalit Model for Praxis-Nexus." *Seminary Ridge Review; Gettysburg* 15, no. 2 (Spring 2013): 64–71.

———. "Visibility of Her Sins. Reading the 'Sinful Woman' in Luke 7:36–50 from a Dalit Feminist Perspective." In *Dalit Theology in the Twenty-First Century: Discordant Voices, Discerning Pathways*, edited by Sathianathan Clarke, Manchala Deenabandhu, and Philip Peacock, 252–265. New Delhi: Oxford University Press, 2010.

Niemandt, Cornelius J. P. "Trends in Missional Ecclesiology." *HTS Teologiese Studies* 68, no. 1 (2012): 1–9.

Nigam, Khuturam Sunani, Ranjana Padhi, and Debaranjan Sarangi. "The Price of Dalit Assertion: On the Burning Down of Dalit Houses in Lathore, OdishaNigam." *Economic and Political Weekly* 47, no. 35 (2012): 19–22.

Nirmal, A. P. "A Dialogue with Dalit Literature." In *Towards a Dalit Theology*, edited by M. E. Prabhakar, 64–82. New Delhi: ISPCK, 1988.

———. "Doing Theology from a Dalit Perspective." In *A Reader in Dalit Theology*, edited by Arvind P. Nirmal, 139–44. Madras, India: Gurukul Lutheran Theological College, 1990.

———. "Towards a Christian Dalit Theology." In *A Reader in Dalit Theology*, edited by Arvind P. Nirmal, 53–70. Madras, India: Gurukul Lutheran Theological College, 1990.

Nyamiti, Charles. "Contemporary African Christologies: Assessment and Practical Suggestions." *Paths of African Theology* (1994): 62–77.

Pai, Sudha. *Dalit Assertion: Oxford India Short Introductions*. 1st ed. New Delhi: Oxford University Press, 2013.

Palmer, Delano, and Dieumeme Noelliste. "Christ and Liberation: Toward a Messianic Christology for a Postcolonial Society." In *Diverse and Creative Voices: Theological Essays from the Majority World*, edited by Sung Wook Chung and Dieumeme Noelliste, 84–101. Havertown, UK: James Clarke, 2015.

Park, A. Sung. "Minjung Theology: A Korean Contextual Theology." *Indian Journal of Theology* 33 (1984): 1–11.

Parratt, John. *An Introduction to Third World Theologies*. Cambridge: Cambridge University Press, 2004.

———. Introduction to *An Introduction to Third World Theologies*, edited by John Parratt, 11–25. Cambridge: Cambridge University Press, 2004.

Patrick, Gnana. *Public Theology: Indian Concerns, Perspectives, and Themes*. Minneapolis: Fortress, 2020.

Phiri, Isabel Apawo. "Southern Africa." In *An Introduction to Third World Theologies*, edited by John Parratt, 137–162. Cambridge: Cambridge University Press, 2004.

Pinnock, Clark H. "Church in the Power of the Holy Spirit: The Promise of Pentecostal Ecclesiology." *Journal of Pentecostal Theology* 14, no. 2 (April 2006): 147–165.

Prabhakar, M. E. "Doing Theology with Poetic Traditions of India with Special Reference to the Dalit Poetry of Poet-Laureate, Joshua." In *Doing Theology with the Poetic Traditions of India: Focus on Dalit and Tribal Poems*, edited by Joseph Patmury, 3–20. Bangalore: PTCA/SATHRI, 1996.

———. "The Search for a Dalit Theology." In *A Reader in Dalit Theology*, edited by Arvind P. Nirmal, 41–51. Madras, India: Gurukul Lutheran Theological College, n.d.

Press Trust of India. "Kerala Assembly Passes Anti-CAA Resolution in Assembly." India Today. Accessed January 20, 2021. https://www.indiatoday.in/india/story/kerala-cm-tables-anti-caa-resolution-in-assembly-1632845-2019-12-31.

Rajkumar, Peniel. *Dalit Theology and Dalit Liberation: Problems, Paradigms and Possibilities*. London: Routledge, 2016.

Rajkumar, Peniel Jesudason Rufus. "A Dalithos Reading of a Markan Exorcism: Mark 5:1–20." *Expository Times* 118, no. 9 (June 1, 2007): 428–435.

Rawat, Ramnarayan. "The Rise of Dalit Studies and Its Impact on the Study of India: An Interview with Historian Ramnarayan Rawat." Historians. Accessed January 27, 2020. https://www.historians.org/publications-and-directories/perspectives-on-history/summer-2016/the-rise-of-dalit-studies-and-its-impact-on-the-study-of-india-an-interview-with-historian-ramnarayan-rawat.

Ray, Ajit. "Widows Are Not for Burning: Christian Missionary Participation in the Abolition of the Sati Rite." In *Sati: Historical and Phenomenological Essays*, edited by Arvind Sharma, 1st ed., 57–65. Delhi: Motilal Banarsidass, 1988.

Robinson, Rowena. "Asian Public Theology: Its Social Location." In *Theology to Go Public*, edited by Felix Wilfred, 1–14. Delhi: ISPCK, 2013.

Romus, D. John. "Public Theology: Perspectives from the Indian Constitution." In *Theology to Go Public*, edited by Felix Wilfred, 129–149. Delhi: ISPCK, 2013.

Sahoo, Sarbeswar. *Pentecostalism and Politics of Conversion in India*. 1st ed. Cambridge: Cambridge University Press, 2018.

Sanyal, Sanjeev. *Land of the Seven Rivers: A Brief History of India's Geography*. New Delhi: Penguin, 2012.

Savarkar, Vinayak Damodar. *Hindutva: Who Is a Hindu?* Bombay, India: Veer Savarkar Prakashan, 1969.

Sebastian, J. Jayakiran. "'Can We Now Bypass That Truth?'—Interrogating the Methodology of Dalit Theology." *Transformation* 25, nos. 2/3 (2008): 80–91.

Sengupta, Nitish K. *Land of Two Rivers: A History of Bengal from the Mahabharata to Mujib*. New Delhi: Penguin, 2011.

Sharan, Ram. "Dalits in India: In Historical Perspective of Caste System." *International Journal of Advanced Research in Management and Social Sciences* 1, no. 5 (2012): 1–8.

Sharma, Arvind. "Sati: A Study in Western Reactions." In *Sati: Historical and Phenomenological Essays*, edited by Arvind Sharma, 1st ed., 1–13. Delhi: Motilal Banarsidass, 1988.

Shiri, Godwin. *Dalit Christians: A Saga of Faith and Pathos*. New Delhi: ISPCK, 2012.

Singh, Ekta. *Caste System in India: A Historical Perspective*. Delhi: Kalpaz, 2005.

Singh, Roja. "Bama's Critical-Constructive Narratives. Interweaving Resisting Visible Bodies and Emancipatory Audacious Voice as TEXTure for Dalit Women's Freedom." In *Dalit Theology in the Twenty-First Century: Discordant Voices, Discerning Pathways*, edited by Sathianathan Clarke, Manchala Deenabandhu, and Philip Peacock, 215–230. New Delhi: Oxford University Press, 2010.

Singh, Santosh K. "The Caste Question and Songs of Protest in Punjab." *Economic and Political Weekly* 52, no. 34 (2017): 33–37.

Skira, Jaroslav Z. "After Our Likeness: The Church as the Image of the Trinity." *Theological Studies* 60, no. 2 (June 1999): 376–377.

Smit, Dirkie. "Notions of the Public and Doing Theology." *International Journal of Public Theology* 1, no. 3 (September 1, 2007): 431–454.

Snell, Jeffrey T. "Beyond the Individual and into the World: A Call to Participation in the Larger Purposes of the Spirit on the Basis of Pentecostal
Theology." *Pneuma* 14, no. 1 (1992): 43–57.

Stackhouse, Max L. "Public Theology and Ethical Judgment." *Theology Today*
54, no. 2 (1997): 165–179.

Stanislaus, L. *The Liberative Mission of the Church among Dalit Christians.* New
Delhi: ISPCK, 1999.

Stewart, John W. "The Shape of the Church: Congregational and Trinitarian."
*Christian Century*, May 20, 1998, 541–542.

Stinton, Diane. "Africa, East and West." In *An Introduction to Third World Theologies*, edited by John Parratt, 105–136. Cambridge: Cambridge University Press, 2004.

Tartakov, Gary Michael. *Dalit Art and Visual Imagery.* New Delhi: Oxford
University Press, 2012.

Teltumbde, Anand. "Azadi Kooch: Towards a New Grammar of the Dalit
Struggle." *Economic and Political Weekly* 52, no. 31 (August 5, 2017):
10–11.

———. *Dalits: Past, Present and Future.* London: Routledge, 2016.

———. "More Than Secularism." *Economic and Political Weekly* 49, no. 19
(2014): 10–11.

Thapar, Romila. "Ethics, Religion, and Social Protest in the First Millennium
B.C. in Northern India." *Daedalus* 104, no. 2 (1975): 119–132.

Thomas, Madathilparampil Mammen. *The Secular Ideologies of India and the
Secular Meaning of Christ.* Confessing the Faith in India Series. Madras,
India: Christian Literature Society, 1976.

Veeneman, Mary M. *Introducing Theological Method: A Survey of Contemporary
Theologians and Approaches.* Grand Rapids, MI: Baker Academic, 2017.
Kindle.

Veli-Matti, Kärkkäinen. *An Introduction to Ecclesiology. Historical, Global, and
Interreligious Perspectives.* Revised and expanded ed. Downers Grove, IL:
IVP Academic, 2021.

Venter, Rian. "Speaking God Today: The Adventures of a Rediscovered Trinitarian Grammar." Inaugural lecture, University of the Free State (UFS),
Bloemfontein, South Africa, April 2011.

Verghese, Paul. *The Secular Ideology: An Impotent Remedy for India's Communal
Problem.* New Delhi: ISPCK, 1998.

Volf, Miroslav. *After Our Likeness: The Church as the Image of the Trinity.* Sacra
Doctrina. Grand Rapids, MI: Eerdmans, 1997.

Webster, John C. B. "From Indian Church to Indian Theology: An Attempt at Theological Construction." In *A Reader in Dalit Theology*, edited by Arvind P. Nirmal, 93–127. Madras, India: Gurukul Lutheran Theological College, n.d.

———. *Religion and Dalit Liberation: An Examination of Perspectives*. 2nd ed. New Delhi: Manohar, 2002.

Whitehead, Henry. *Work among Indian Outcastes*. London: Society for Promoting Christian Knowledge, 1912.

Wilfred, Felix. "On the Future of Asian Theology: Public Theologizing." In *Theology to Go Public*, edited by Felix Wilfred, 28–55. Delhi: ISPCK, 2013.

Williams, Byron. "Prophetic Public Theology." *Review & Expositor* 111, no. 2 (May 2014): 159–170.

Williams, Monier. *A Sanskrit-English Dictionary: Etymologically and Philologically Arranged with Special Reference to Cognate Indo-European Languages*. New Delhi: Motilal Banarsidass, 1899.

Wilson, K. "Towards a Humane Culture." In *A Reader in Dalit Theology*, edited by Arvind P. Nirmal, 151–168. Madras, India: Gurukul Lutheran Theological College, 1990.

Wright, Christopher J. H. *The Mission of God: Unlocking the Bible's Grand Narrative*. Downers Grove, IL: IVP Academic, 2006.

Zokoue, Isaac. "The Church as Pneumatic Community: Toward an Ecclesiology for the African Context." In *Diverse and Creative Voices: Theological Essays from the Majority World*, edited by Sung Wook Chung and Dieumeme Noelliste, 143–159. Havertown, UK: James Clarke, 2015.

# Subject Index

# Scripture Index